They mate back-to-back; the abdominal clasp is very strong

The distinction between butterfl... and moths is not a clear one

The butterfly's watchspring-like tongue is called the 'proboscis'

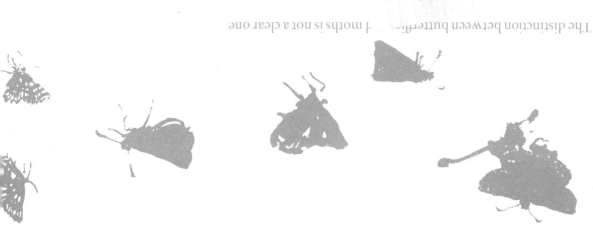

The 'imago' is the butterfly stage of the life-cycle, as distinct from egg, larva, or pupa

hindwing

abdomen

thorax

head

clubbed antennae

compound eyes

forewing

BRIGHT WINGS OF SUMMER

BRIGHT WINGS OF SUMMER
Watching Butterflies

David G. Measures

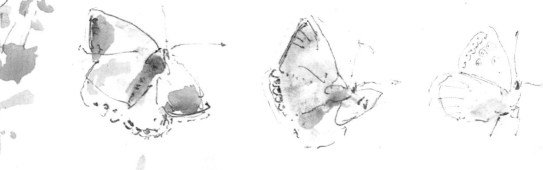

PRENTICE~HALL, INC.
glewood Cliffs, N.J.

dull insitting in the grass.

clouded yellow flew past &
settled on yellow parsnip.

skippers with black antennae
feeding from scabious or the
large ragged knapweed head
then resting on the stem of
a long grass. dark green settled
A worn silvers. until lay
afternoon getting warmer &
sun now & then thro' the haze
A continual fly past of insects

CONTENTS

Forewords

As a painter and naturalist myself, as an intermittent nature diarist, as a lepidopterist since youth who never had a collection of dead insects and as President of the British Butterfly Conservation Society, I welcome David Measures' book with admiration and enthusiasm.

For most of perhaps four million years as a distinct species, man has pitted his wits and bent his energies against nature. Only very recently has he begun to accept the inescapable scientific facts that he is a part of nature and that all nature is inter-related. Human nature can change only at the infinitesimally slow rate of evolutionary change, which, of course, varies from species to species of animal or plant, and may have been a little more rapid in man than in many others. But human attitudes are something different. They can and do change much faster. One of Chekhov's characters declared that he would turn over a new leaf and from thenceforward, to show that he was basically an enlightened and worthy person, he would spend his life cutting down the forests and draining the marshes. In many parts of the world such an objective would not now be regarded as enlightened or worthy (though in others it still might be). The concept of mankind learning to coexist with wild nature — in spite of the relentless and ever-increasing human pressures on the finite land areas of our planet — is relatively new, but seems to be gaining ground encouragingly. It is a concept to which this book makes an important contribution. The principles that have guided the author's rare insight into the aesthetic beauty, scientific interest and philosophic delight of studying living butterflies can as well be applied, as he himself points out, to any amateur observations of the natural world.

It is a real pleasure to be allowed to contribute a foreword to this book and to wish it success. It carries a vital message.

PETER SCOTT
Slimbridge

I am a scientist and as such endeavour to measure natural phenomena in an attempt to understand them. David Measures is an artist and as such records natural phenomena in his own special way in an attempt to communicate his understanding to others.

For almost a decade he has made it his business to study the vibrant life of the insects along a stretch of disused railway line near Southwell in Nottinghamshire. Some of the results of his immense and detailed records are presented in this book. Each of his sketches is woven into a matrix of accurately recorded fact, each page lives, a perfect amalgam of art and science. His is both total art and total science, a renaissance in which new life is given to both disciplines and a new understanding to the subject of insect ecology.

Since working in the field with David I have begun to look at living organisms in a new way. I let the plants and animals I study both ask and answer the questions; my part is as an observer.

Bright Wings of Summer will open up this whole new world of experience to you, a world that exists just on the other side of your double glazing. It is a world that will answer as many questions as it poses, the depth of the answers being in proportion to the time you are willing to invest in observation.

DAVID J. BELLAMY
Durham

Acknowledgements

Were it not for David Bellamy this book would never have been conceived. It was David who persuaded me to join him on one of his television programmes to tell people about the natural potential of disused railway tracks, how I came to discover this, respond to it, and how every year I became more fascinated, as it too increased in its natural richness. Through his television work David Bellamy has made accessible an understanding of the natural world to a wide audience. Above all, for me, he demonstrated a means of making sense of this bewildering detail, variety and shift.

It was seven years ago that I met John Heath, and his continued help and encouragement confirmed for me the value of what I was doing.

My thanks are also due to the following:

All my friends who have helped me over the years of my interest in butterflies, and especially my wife and children, who have shared the difficulties along with the pleasures of the fieldwork. (My wife's drawings of the poplar hawk moth are shown on pages 64–5.)

John Morgan for his photography, his continued interest and assistance.

Mrs Ruth Robinson for typing and helping me correct and piece together the parts of the text.

Dr Clarke (Zoological Dept, Nottingham University) for his professional consultations.

Lastly, the staff of Walter Parrish International — to Tim Auger, Rick Fawcett, and above all Mrs Phoebe Phillips, who seemed so well to understand the lure of working in the wild, and who with calm assurance succeeded in getting a text from me in what seemed an impossibly short time.

DAVID G. MEASURES
Southwell

11

Introduction

Until ten years ago, I was no more interested in butterflies than anyone else. Yet it was because I had a bicycle which I used daily to travel the three miles from my home down into the valley, to the nearest local railway station, that I first became aware that a small, copper-coloured butterfly I occasionally glimpsed on the way was not a common sight in over-farmed Nottinghamshire.

Cycling is a most satisfying everyday activity. Anyone seeing me in the morning tearing along late might wonder at this, but the journey home at the end of the day is a different matter. Whim and weather permitting, there is time then to banish tension and watch, piece together how we as humans fit into our land, the land that is like a clock for anyone who will read the signs in their punctual recurrence.

I had always been intrigued by the changes in the landscape of the familiar route that each week brought throughout the year, and its speed and extent of change — incredible. In May sunshine the new, fresh, green growth of meadow can change to a field of whiteness — cow parsley and hawthorn blossom — so that from the train window it is possible to imagine a snow-covering in late spring.

This book is for people who care about life – our own and that of the other creatures that live with us. It so happened that butterflies became the focus of my recent work but any other study of the integration of wildness would yield results just as absorbing.

Butterflies are big, showy insects: most people recognize at least one or two, or at the very least have watched their brilliantly patterned, fluttering wings with delight and pleasure. Their present scarcity should act as an indicator of an all-round reduction. My next-door neighbour tells me that it was a normal sight, and only thirty years ago, for the Common Blue to rise in abundance as she walked across the meadow into the village at buttercup time. Then came World War II, and meadows went to the plough, destroying the food plant of the larvae.

Theirs is now a common fate — many other insects less conspicuous, yet equally intriguing and useful, as well as birds, mammals and flowers, are ousted from haunts all over developed countries as present-day farming methods and annual building programmes encroach. Somehow, perhaps because of their very beauty and brilliance, butterflies have been particularly vulnerable. What has not been done inadvertently has been done deliberately, in the name of collection for amateur pleasure and professional profit.

Let me show you how I arrived at an understanding of the world of living butterflies through drawing, note-taking and photography, in place of dead examples in a cabinet. I have gained such extraordinary satisfaction from my encounters with living butterflies that I hope you will be encouraged to find a similar joy for yourself. And the notes that I have made for this past ten years which are summarized in the second part of the book may serve as an introduction to communication between insects and that close-knit relationship with their habitat which Lawrence Durrell has characterized in human terms as 'The Spirit of Place'.

How necessary it is to urge lepidopterists to relinquish their old habits of collecting. How many ornithologists today would think of going out on a normal bird-watching excursion with the intention of capturing and killing the objects of their interest? The very idea is preposterous. Yet most butterfly-hunters still use their skills for killing.

It is true that superb collections have been made in the past. Variations according to latitude and district have been established; comparative distribution, the charting and comparison of yesterday's records with today's sightings are well in hand. And of course some specimen-collecting may still have importance in establishing new species, or other scientific programmes. But almost all present-day collecting is basically for the personal pleasure of display, and it is a wry thought that once the population of a particular species is endangered by any one of a dozen reasons, the very people who show the greatest interest are the keenest collectors, anxious to ensure a specimen for their cabinet, thus ensuring even quicker disappearance and the loss of any further chance of adaptation or survival.

In the past, we did not fully understand how drastically such enthusiasm, understandable in itself, can damage the whole abundance of insects, birds, mammals and flowers. Now we *do* know — we have been shown, over and over again, the effects of our thoughtlessness. And we are changing. More and more research is done in the field, or at the very least with living animals closely observed in a controlled environment — living animals, living butterflies.

Collectors learn the importance of stalking, remaining quiet and unnoticed until within reach of observation and notation. But the net and the killing bottle turn a living creature into a carcass, unworthy of further study except for dissection or identification. How much better to stalk, sit and make notes, to wait or watch for life instead of death.

The lure of watching butterflies is that they are day-flying and sun-loving, and I find it is exceedingly pleasurable to be outside and to take part in the zestful business of living.

For those of us without resources of microscopes and specialist equipment, it seems sensible to choose for study big insects which can be noticed easily and so kept under scrutiny; and of course butterfly markings and colour variations are visually satisfying.

Working only out of doors and only from life, my drawings are intended to note the activity of the insect rather than make a picture of it. It is neither relevant to make a finished drawing nor is there any need; there are many excellent painted facsimiles. The pleasure is in being outside and taking part in its life and daily experience. A page of notes covering perhaps two hours in time has a strong feel of place and time, even though it consists only of jottings, and a few sketches. I have learned over the years to increase the accuracy and depth of my notes, and from early incidents and later observations I try to piece together the meaning and pattern of butterflies' relationships throughout their life-span. The drawings in colour and black-and-white are all taken from my diaries, dating back to 1966. They are my way of recording my response, a form of visual shorthand, and although I hope they convey something of the pleasure and delight I have found, I am sure other people find their own ways of recording which are just as satisfying.

Today, a study of the living insect is the sort of work that the amateur can do best — written observations from long periods of time spent in the field, with all the advantages that leisure, chance and whim give him over the professional who is usually out to test a particular aspect of study in a quantitative manner.

Eye-witness accounts of the field behaviour of butterflies are difficult to come by. Even in the science libraries, with a few exceptions, the best that can be found are mere anecdotes, a single line or two. There are so many questions to be answered about imago adult behaviour — where can you find out about a selection of flowers (does there seem to be a colour or scent preference?), the relationship one species has with another, dominance, territory behaviour, bird predation of the adult butterfly, the likely predator for a certain species in a certain locality and how the butterfly responds to changes caused by man's presence?

Courtship in the wild (the field and forest), as distinct from courtship in captivity, is an aspect difficult to plan for and impossible to control, a good reason why it has been neglected by the professional until recently. It is this quality of the impossible and unknown which gives a study in the field its attraction.

The act of courtship is the rarest sight of all. It may happen only on one or two days in the entire year, and to witness it is the result of very good fortune and/or very careful planning! To capture that moment on film or photograph is no easy task, and to note down an idea of it on paper is almost impossible, as the event is over too quickly. Once pairing takes place (*and* you happen to be there at the time, *and* with pencil and/or camera) then recording it is a more straightforward task, for it can take anything up to an hour. Text books tell us little, and what they do offer is almost entirely based on captive breeding; and so their accounts lack the authenticity and spice of the wild, and the critical association with the selected site and conditions.

Of course, there is no doubt that to make a truly complete and fully accurate picture of the ecology of an insect or a site is possible only for the trained scientist with all the resources of funds, laboratory assistance and team work. In the natural sciences today, big issues are out of the hands of the amateur and the individual. Remember (and not so long ago) the efforts needed to overcome the locust problem — a considerable team worked at it over a period of eight years. Any aspect of ecology that is as tied in with man's economy as the locust will usually find money and backing for research.

Nevertheless, it seems to me very necessary and quite feasible that

every naturalist, trained or self-taught like myself, should tease out for himself some understanding of a chosen place, however small, however limited. By patient observation over a period of years we can assess its make-up, flux, and shifts.

In the following pages, I shall describe my own experiences and studies in the English countryside. But the ideas and patterns are there as models, as a background for whatever you find in your own neighbourhood, wherever you live. For butterflies occur from the Arctic to the tropics. Most of the butterflies near my home have nearly identical or related sub-species in Alaska, North and South America, North Africa and Asia. The Small White, for example, is found in many parts of the world. Others, like the Large Heath and the Castle Eden Dene Blue, are so locked into micro-climates and local conditions that they vary in markings from colony to colony, even when the colonies are separated by only a mile or two. At the outset, most basic identification books will give you typical examples of your local species. But no two butterflies are identical, even of the same species, so it is ultimately up to you, with experience and patience, to distinguish and note down individuals so that you can observe behaviour with accuracy.

Whatever the deficiencies of such a rough study in terms of the quantitative and repeated result required by science, one's own experience more than compensates for these shortcomings in offering an unending and satisfying pursuit, the substance of which is never exhausted while we live.

orange tip
clinging to
goose grass in
damp ditch
7 P.m. 22·5·67

PART ONE:
BEGINNINGS

Down by the sea, a relaxed mood is slowly created by sunshine and saltern; we have time to idle, watch, and dream. Ears are lulled with piping of redshank and even the calling of distant children as they fish. Out in the vast open sky and sea, the landscape absorbs all sharpness of human sounds. You look for a place to relax — and if you are observant you will notice that the places you select for their warmth and comfort are similarly occupied by the greatest variety of flowers and insects.

Further out towards the sea, the high tide slaps the walls and the cleansing wind blows the tough marram and sea spinach. But a little behind the exposed outer shore, a tangle of briar and stunted thorn has intergrown with saltmarsh rush, pushing through like thick hair, brushed by the winds, bouncy and resilient. Where the south-east-facing hollows radiate the maximum sun, close to thickets and grass, there, you may find a Gatekeeper — the Hedge Brown butterfly with its twin eye spot. It is here, in preference to all other sites, that the first Gatekeeper appears, newly emerged, damp velvet and glowing as it lies spread to the sun, protected from the cold wind that holds the others of its species back in their pupa cases. It was one of these that ten years ago I idly painted, my very first sketch of a butterfly that bewitched me then and has done ever since.

In the lee of the raised causeway there is a swathe of fine grasses between marram bank and the fence of the grazed meadow, and here one can wander and abandon oneself. There is a footpath along the tidal dyke where wild carrot and vetches bloom amid bleached turf, the colour of silver sand. And butterflies. I began to realize what colour and shifting brilliance the butterfly wears on its wings — the vibrance of the Blues, and the iridescence of the Small Copper.

There is a magnet in me drawn to the subtle sense-aura of wild freedom, the porous exchange apparent outside in wild places and the richness of variety and subtlety which I miss inside a building. It tones the senses and gives a more-than-human confidence, sharpens awareness, adroitness and decision.

Early Man the hunter not only filled his belly, but fulfilled himself; he not only established and handed on a craft of survival, he partook of the spirit of living, becoming more than mere Man. Today, with the increased sterility of architecture and our allotted space in a functioning unit, we have a need for wilderness as never before.

When I was a child my home was the Old Toll Cottage and its old fashioned garden stretching down to the River Avon, lying beneath Warwick Castle. All of my childhood was very close to the earth — I had a plot for myself with quantities of lilies and sea holly — and like every child I was fascinated by all natural things. I made drawings of birds I saw from the garden and riverbank, my first attempts, from the age of seven, at drawing out of doors.

The old bridges ran immediately off our riverbank, with the mill-pond downstream. As soon as we could swim, my sister and I had a free run of the river, the waterfalls, and the island. On summer mornings, before breakfast, school or work, we would wander down to the river and swim among the reddish, feathery rootlets, so clear in the running water. I was allowed extraordinary freedom of the river from the age of seven, to take off alone with a boat, to row up the river even in the thickest fogs, to wander and swim under the weir. I would climb down and sit underneath the waterfall, or swim in among all the turmoil of the water with the pink-finned roaches, who were waiting for the fresh food supply that came tumbling over the weir. I would float up to them, head into the water as they did. It was a curious feeling as they touched against my skin.

We were used to the three weirs. Annually we would clear them of the winter débris so that during summer there was a clean fall of water. Sometimes I would sit under the cascade and block my ears with my fingers, normal senses cut off by the din of the water.

Swimming alone without splash or noise, I could approach living creatures as part of their environment, watching dabchicks and moorhens and the annual influx of sandpipers, without the aid of field glasses.

I discovered the natural world mostly on my own, for when I was with friends normal activity was noisy and communal. It still seems

31·7·69
Nettlecombe
valley
h·t sunny a/t.
3 sitings

underside of ♂ purple hairstreak (captive)
- this spec. caught on ragwort, top of small hill;
another seen on bracken; the third on brambles

1·8·69   Another flying across the lawn
at 8 pm & appeared to settle on the side
of house or in the magnolia tree.

Large skippers at gate entrance, gamboling then feeding from rosebay, moving from flower
flower — now 4 of 5 cocks! Also resting / feeding on St John's wort. A hen on a bramble
leaf

occasional
thly coloured ♂

and from
blue cranesbill

and from bramble
flowers

feeding from thistle

Some of the skippers seem
to be visitor population
feeding from willow herb.
in ups & off across the hawthorn
...s

...s a small heath appeared
at the grassy entrance : a good
..ay from its area of track where
..st prolific.

...re white being chased off
... m. brown..

..e skippers don't seem to
...ther with m. brown, & it
... happen upon one settled
...either give any sign of
...cognition. Another skipper in the
...a & its off like an arrow

..ll marked small heath will
...upt its search for chickweed
..lazily bob at a m. brown &
...versa

The cocks can be very
dull coloured & dingy &
more like honey bee
It is the hen which has
the vaseline green tinge
As they dash past
twirl in a threesome
The wings seem to revolve
like a toy aeroplane whirring
past pulled by its propellor

24th

blue chasing with a hedge brown
The hedge brown is rather small
compared with meadow brown
& looks like a larger
version of the s. heath.

A cock fed from meadow sweet

hen feeding from
ragwort flowers
& sunning on
bramble leaves

and later feeding
from thyme on path

two sway
heath
wandered
into the ragwort patch
a brief rest & wandered
back again one stopping for
feed at the ragwort flowers

alight for
on path
The cocks are timid &
unapproachable

The cocks barely
settle but hover as
if about to alight
in this warm clear
afternoon sun. They are smaller
darker than the hens who feed
contentedly from the fine
ragwort heads on the hillside

In the clearer sunshine of this
to yesterday's, the fritillaries are
noticeably feeding from thistle
direct flight paths to the flow

A hen
meadow
brown
feeding
on ragwort
with here
gatekeepers
more grey &
less round

resting briefly
in grasses

hen resting on
cranesbill
later in
afternoon,
butterflies
no longer feeding
from ragwort

The shadows are long, the sun still clear & bright
6 p.m.

necessary for the observation of nature to be a solitary activity if one is to develop a sufficient depth of awareness.

When I take my own children with me, it is different because they have grown up knowing they have to be quiet, enjoying things on their own without the need to talk. Off in the early morning sun, it is marvellous when everything is still, quiet and fresh, creatures appearing slow and sunning in the first warmth. We take our drawing things and camera. I must admit that I prefer drawing, yet there are times when photographic records are necessary. So there we are, each in a different spot, working within hailing distance and alerting each other when one of our insect characters is on the move. It is surprising at how early an age children can be completely enthralled by this kind of activity — Sally started coming with me as a four-year-old. She is quite at home in the countryside and if I miss something she, with her young, sharp eyes, is quick to point it out. She quickly learned to identify species and that is a great help; I can concentrate on getting my observations down on paper as they tell me what else is going on. Children maintain their interest for a long time, if they are enjoying their occupation. For them it is very exciting to see real drama like the spider and the Common Blue hen (on page 127) — that sort of incident once seen is never forgotten.

Each fights for a turn with the camera. Once I have adjusted it to the day's conditions they quite happily go off and stalk with patience and persistence and come back with great excitement if they think they have got some good shots. Sometimes the sharpness of their slides falls short of our standards but it is surprising how good some of them can be.

Simon is more interested in animals, reptiles and birds than in butterflies. In the New Forest there is a good bit of heathland and gorse, and some old army huts. Butterflies like the reflected warmth of the concrete bases, which become baking hot, and this is also the perfect place for adders. There are often three or four adders lying together, and you must stalk them very quietly. A single snap of dried bramble and they slither away. Half the fun is to take your sketch pad with you, and try to draw the adders. If you move slowly, they are aware of your presence but do not seem to mind, at least for a few minutes. Sometimes you are lucky enough to see them sloughing their skin, and this great, long, transparent ribbon is Simon's trophy to add, with his drawing, to his collection on his bedroom wall.

All of us work together. It is a great advantage having a wife who can draw too, so that when I have to get off in a hurry, just as one of the pupa cases begins to hatch, Christine, with less teaching commitment than I, takes over. Where our drawings of hatching eggs and developing larvae appear on the same sheet, initially there is little to distinguish hers from mine; in fact they are more delicate.

Everyone today is made aware of environmental conservation. This must be as a result of the many popular and excellent wildlife programmes on television. In my day there were no such advantages — we had to find out for ourselves. But in my childhood butterfly collecting was an accepted hobby. And yes, I did have a killing bottle (something brown-staining and set under plaster of Paris in a screw-top jar). Over some years a boy's crude collection was made.

Yet I insist the most vivid of those butterfly memories was the love of being out of doors in the summer sun. I remember the cross roads at Harbury where we went for Sunday picnics. It was rare in those days for a car to pass the four wide verges of summer flowers where we chased the velvety-black Ringlet. Sometimes we came across one with the absence of an eye mark on the top surface, an expanse of black which was not to be found illustrated in my Saunders butterfly handbook: that always puzzled me.

There too was a stream, lost beneath an arching tangle of bramble and dog-rose, where the growth of the hedge met with the flowers of the verges. Paddling downstream in dappling sun, between its mossy banks, I remember the rich beauty of my first three moths — the Mother Shipton, the Yellow Shell and the pink triangles of the Blood Veins.

I remember how different was my experience of scale in my childhood. Those four verges seemed vast. These days when I see the midget Small Copper butterfly in its super rapid flight, I am reminded that before it emerged as an adult it too experienced a different scale of being. A tiny egg laid on a shred of leaf on which as a larva it moved with infinite slowness, and all within a few inches. The recollection of such a universe within a few feet is a valuable scale when I make charts of their territories. A month can seem a lifetime to a young child — it can be a lifetime to a butterfly.

At school biology fascinated me. The staff in a quiet, capable way nurtured my enthusiasm. Over and above the required course work, the desire on my part was ever present to explore the question — what is that essential bit, the bit we cannot explain, that quality of life which imbues the multitude of separate physical forms. Drawing was a vital part of my involvement. The head game-keeper of the castle park became a good friend to me. Assisting with the monthly duck count of the Wild Fowl Trust, I had been given permission to roam the extent of the park. Between these counts there were mornings when I stalked the wigeon flocks and painted them as close as I could get. On others, from the edges of the wooded lake, I would be after teal, or I would spend an hour watching a solitary, skulking water-rail. He taught me about the game-keeper's job, maintaining, to him, the right balance between reared stocks and 'vermin'. Some of his carcasses provided me with useful comparisons between predators as well as unlimited drawing material.

By the time I went to art-school, I possibly upset some of the models by bringing in dead specimens to dissect during their rests. My principal made an exception for such interests and arranged for the local mortuary to keep a fine badger, part-dissected, whilst I had to be away for a few days. (He also arranged with the county pathologist for me to attend and draw at an autopsy.)

I turned down an opportunity to train as a medical illustrator at Guy's Hospital for, in spite of allowing the application of two skills, it offered no exploration of either biology or painting in a pure sense. So from then on I concentrated on painting and continued at the Slade School of Fine Art. Being so country-orientated I was apprehensive how I would find city life, and was surprised how much wild life there is in London. Since modern intensive farming has depleted much of the countryside, it is in fact the big cities which have the bits of waste ground, near railways and industries, and the odd building sites which have not been redeveloped. For the naturalist, of course, it is ideal to have all these bits of untidiness; they are the reservoir of the future.

London, to my huge surprise, not only had the richness of cultural life of the capital city — it also contained surprising species. I was living out in the suburbs, and one warm, summer's evening we had a swarm of huge black stag-beetles. They take years to grow through their larval and pupal states, so I was amazed at the huge quantity whirring around like great, heavy bi-planes, settling onto the trunks of lime trees where the males outnumbered the females so that there were several males clambering over each in their competition to mate.

My two years at the Slade showed me as never before the potential and demands of painting, as real as any interest in the natural world. The big forces, the ebb and flow of tide and time, the relationship of humanity to the land — the understandable preoccupations of people involved in art — offered the sustaining material which carries most of us through personal change and prevailing influences.

So from my London days, when the grandeur and panache of American painting held sway, to the time when I got to Nottingham, when its influence gradually waned, there was a swing away from the production of an artifact as a momentous object. For me this brought an equally stimulating need to find out more about perception and an understanding of the visual world.

My outlet was through an enjoyment of playing games with the natural forces of the physical world. Through observation I treated my experiences as a set of crossword puzzles to be solved. Each physical change once witnessed supplied a clue, and it was up to me to find some solution. In fact each attempt and each new set of provocations were contained in a new piece of work.

There never seems any simple explanation for changes and new directions. No matter how overt the change in a person's work appears to be, there is a constant underlying drive and interest.

I became more preoccupied with looking into the experience of colour itself. I came across J. C. Rose's demonstrations of the effects of forces on plant growth, and these stimulated me to attempt an understanding of the part colour plays in indicating the state or condition of living things. I tried to find how the colour of a substance reacts to external forces. Basic earth materials, metallic salts, natural dyestuffs, the most old-fashioned of substances, as well as those of our sophisticated culture, such as chemiluminescents, and materials sensitive to change by pressure, heat, moisture and light, provided my test pieces. Why was I doing this? Out of a desire to find out, to know if there were recurring patterns in more areas of the natural world than we know about. Even in human applied colour choice, tendencies to think of colour in certain ways seem to crop up again and again.

For painters there has always been a special quality attached to the way light affects a place, how too the character of morning, noon and evening light gives a special quality.

Because of my work with colour, I began to notice butterflies.

whilst ♀ watched 10 mins pairing
in which they moved around
may then parted   ♂ moving away 1st
10-30   arsed   ♀ remaining quiet

There is nothing so brilliant or as changing and shifting as the
iridescence and the pigmented colour of the butterfly's wing. I began
to keep a visual record. The diary itself, on which most of this book is
based, developed over the years from the time when I first made
notes about these colours. I started in 1966, producing really a loose
notation — flashes of colour mostly, flowers, grasses and butterflies.

I began to wonder why butterflies close up, why they chase each
other, where they go at night, how they communicate, and what
happens in rain. These were questions which had never occurred to
me as a child butterfly-hunter. As an adult watching as the result of
a visual training, the more I drew, the more I wanted to know, so a
written account of what I saw began to take place very naturally at
the sides of the drawings. What I failed to get down in the drawings
on the spot was never worth filling in afterwards, for it lacked that
living response, a sense of immediacy, activity, and the busyness of
the insect.

You have to work quickly; the result is sometimes scribbles, but
the whole of my drawings has to do with taking what is there on the
spot. To try to colour them in or improve them afterwards is useless
— they become dead, dull and lifeless.

A child's multi-colour ballpoint pen is useful — it enables me to
write with the same tool with which I hatch a coloured area. I try to
cut down to a minimum the items carried. For me these comprise

ballpoint, drawing-pad, water-colours and camera, with an apple or orange to quench my thirst. I have learnt to do without a brush and water, and use spit to colour, with my fingers, most of the drawings. A watercolour box is all you need; mine is very small. In a standard product the range of colour is too limited; I add extra colours to the box by filling up the brush space from tubes of pure pigment. Butterfly wings are very brilliant, and there is no time to mix colours on the spot. Occasionally I mix them on the page with a finger. Artist's water-colours are often toxic, so you must not put your finger back in your mouth; just moisten one finger each time. The use of fingers can be surprisingly accurate and the detail of dots can be made with the little fingernail.

As the year goes on the pages improve: skill and confidence grow with the urgency of a new season. The work in each drawing is a direct reflection of the amount of time taken. If the weather has been dull, and the butterflies have been inactive, the the result is a careful and detailed drawing; if it is very hot and the butterflies active, I have either got nothing at all or the merest scribbles.

For me, through watching butterflies, a new world was revealed, supplying, as well as interest, surprise, amusement and admiration. What an advantage this sort of enquiry has over any with a net for it requires a period of standing still. It is impossible to stress too much the importance of this suspension of movement. Even in ordinary everyday life impressions rely on movement to an amazing degree. Something static is almost always secondary to your attention, and for all the rest of macro-living beings, the same is true. While you are moving, and especially moving vigorously, everything else will be well aware of the spectacle, and slip, unnoticed, out of your way.

Then I find occasionally something extra can take place in the relationship between me and it. I speak of the rare time that occurs when after a period of watching, your particular butterfly character appears to come to terms with you. Reconciled to your presence, it seems to allow a trust to exist, whereby both of you take part, each functioning in your own way, freely and co-existent.

Think of the wealth of life performing in front of your gaze in each and every spot. There are far too many insects other than butterflies that catch your attention. The next decision that I had to make was on what to concentrate. So I selected only those that I noticed impinged directly in some way on the butterflies. These included examples of the hoverflies, bumbles, crickets and day-flying moths.

It is on such occasions that a camera is invaluable because the encounter between butterfly and insect is so rapid that it is impossible to get it down on paper. I find photography is more

cumbersome so it has remained a secondary activity, never quite as
enjoyable as working with pen and paper — too many machines,
too much to be adjusted, looked at, re-adjusted, posed and wound
up. In a practical sense I still find the camera viewfinder restricts the
naturally much wider extent of human vision. So even with my
other eye open I often 'lose' the insect if it flies off. It was a good day
then, last July, when I found that John Morgan, a photographer and
colleague at the art school where I teach, was willing to come and do
the lion's share of the camera work for me. I had expected that he
would be bored after the first half hour spent watching one species.
It turned out that he was deeply interested, and we have worked
together successfully ever since. Now, when two butterflies part, we
have already decided who will follow the hen and who the cock. I
am drawing and writing furiously whilst John is filming and the final
write-up and interpretation can be discussed and verified. The result
is an expanded and more complete picture of what really goes on.
For all his help, and another pair of eyes, I am grateful.

I may have given the impression that watching butterflies is all
one long idyll. Not a bit of it: there is never any certainty in watching
butterflies. Something interesting happens when you least expect it.
Usually towards the end of the afternoon, just as I have got to the last
frame of my film, I am out of paper, my family have arranged to
meet me and I am very weary, the action that I have been waiting for
the whole day is taking place before my eyes.

This is not the end of my troubles either, for often in the heat of
the moment, pursuing an unknown butterfly in flight, it is quite
likely I have entered someone's private property.

32

Oct 11. 30   2 torts on hebe   1 on parsley wall   sunshine now more
on Michaelmas daisy   3 torts fading out   + honey bees (nine in all)
(torts)

comma suddenly
appeared at ¼ to 12
on hebe

8 RFL   Tuesday 29th August

0 Am   Wan misty sun .   a slight cooling breeze

Adonis blue ♂   whizzes about & feeding on valerian
sitting wings open   gatekeepers & m. browns in teagrass
fragment of   in the dell   already some feeding
nectar .

gatekeeper

only ♀'s feeding &
they have different
amounts of
orange on
the u.r top
forewings.   ♀ wall came down to feed
                    10.25 a moment of sunshine
                    & the common blue
                    10.30 . adonis ♂ came over into dell
                    & almost settled on majoram
                    10.40
                    adonis feeding on the majoram
                    10.50   marbled white feeding in
                    this gentle sun &

'1.15   adonis ♂
feeding solidly from
majoram

a small tort. joined the
m. browns to feed from
large maj clumps.
11.2
small coppers
& lulworth skippers
feeding from   majoram.

chalkhill
pauses a moment
on an old selfheal perch

By now the chalkhill cock
is parading the dell.
the midget brown argus are
wandering the surface of the vegetation
of the dell

Adonis ♂ comes down to base of dell
to feed. closely s. copper &

11.30   s. coppers nosing each other again
this time the & & & & & & &

The 2 small coppers feeding close beside each other
the are quivering & walking down the stem of maj head
visiting certain   ♂ seems only mildly interested in
her who has climbed onto old stick on her own & gives up
& goes & walks to flower head to feed.

common blue)
feeding from wild
5-30. thyme x
sour thistle

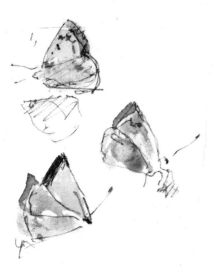

On a Welsh holiday, armed with a permit in the well-wardened Llandwyn Reserve, I was standing painting, stock still in the heather, and overheard two women entering by the public path. They looked across at me and one observed to her companion, 'I didn't know they had scarecrows in nature reserves!' Admittedly it was on a scorchingly hot summer day, and there I was, wrapped up in overcoat, scarf and hat, recovering after an illness. I cocked my eye and smiled to myself.

A much worse experience took place on a hot summer's day in the New Forest. It may sound ridiculous, but not being used to handling horses, I was sufficiently frightened to get out of their field as best I could. I could see two horses in the far distance when I entered the pasture, and then thought no more about them. I was busy chasing a blue, which I lost in mid-air to a great aeshna dragon-fly, then I turned back up a little stream to follow a Cinnabar and was painting away when the two horses came springing up, their ears down and their manes flying. They snorted and had a wicked look in their eyes, and were obviously displeased at my presence. I tried ignoring them but it made no difference. They came up either side and shouldered me, leant in and pushed down heavily on me, a crushing which physically was no joke. Escape I did, Cinnabar forgotten, but the lick

×1½

the same red tinged
dragonfly as a
Fiskerton track

a me.. speckled wood closer to cottage,
also very pale/white spots
but more handsome, velvety +
larger hindwing spots

×2

morning warming +
s. wood no longer sunny

of a tongue had smeared the crimson across the page, showing
anybody who doubts the tale.

It is not always at the time when you are out butterflying that the
real significance of your watching is realised. Your attention may be
drawn by something present in a completely different situation, out
of which springs an idea. Through it occurs a different way of
understanding the relationship of the parts.

Over a number of seasons' watching I began to realise that the activity of butterflies shifts from one place to another, according to the time of day and the direction of the sun. Put like this it sounds a very ordinary statement and only to be expected. But then a simile occurred which seemed to bring it to life — that this shifting insect activity zone is not dissimilar to the edge of a tide. Through butterflies and from any one point I was witnessing the peak activity at the edge of the sun's tide as it shifts across the land. The following illustration shows how this thought occurred. I was walking across a causeway so pitted with rock pools and unevenly eroded that the route has to be selected, every foot placed with decision, in spite of a discernible well-worn track. For every slippery, algae-covered stone or patch of seaweed there is an alternative barnacled surface, so the walk across is not so much difficult as slow. Across I went to the welcome turf slopes of the island, with time only for a brief visit before having to return or be cut off by the late afternoon tide. In the narrowest and lowest part of the causeway, the birds collected. They thronged the rocks; gulls, oyster catchers, turnstones, ringed plover and other little waders were dibbing and running before the rising waterline. The tide was pulsing from both sides of the ford, gradually swelling to mix, merge and cover the ground completely.

Obviously there must be an extra-rich supply of fresh food to attract such an influx of birds, yet I had never troubled to get to know exactly what it was. So on the safe side of the diminishing path, I squatted to watch a rock pool in one of the main tide-channels. As the tide spills in extra water, the shrimps, small grey spotted fish and little black ones too, all rise at the edges of the rock pool to the new water mark. Each rushing infill is followed by a gentle ebbing overspill, so for the newly wet barnacles there is a short period when an alternating supply of cold surf occurs: a sudden gush then a gentle ebb. The crustacea and fish rising with the water mark graze the sides and deftly pick up morsels of crushed barnacle. Each is careful not to be stranded as the water sinks, although the next wave is not long bringing a fresh bath — and a quick exit to any that are careless!

The incoming tide must be real release to the shoal of elvers and pollack, confined in a pool increasingly tepid and stagnant, dashing frantically away from the glancing touch of anemone tentacles. Those that are caught are pulled right down, often head first, into the depth of the muscular jelly orb. The streamlined silver-perfection of the fish, this quality of resilience of the living is quickly disturbed and

damaged by the sucking digestive juices of the tentacles sapping them to death. Curious that the very fish that themselves scavenge are at the mercy of static adventurers lacking their advantages of free movement. And they in turn are nourished and betrayed by the tide which gives them added food, attracting birds which feed avidly on the fresh plankton and newly-fed fish.

We too take part in this shifting, elemental ebb and flow. I must decide whether to be stranded, or hasten back to safety and to others of my kind. We sit safely ashore to witness the quick changing flood, with some awe at such dimensions. First the gathering and shifting of the flocks, and hidden from afar, but clearly there, the swimming and wading life moving and flickering before the greedily wetting swell.

This inexorable flow of the tidal pulse is expressed throughout the living world. The general pattern of change is well known, the means and instances of fulfilling this are endlessly intriguing.

From the myriad diversity each rallies its own kind, grouping then remixing, for a moment achieving dominance, then slipping away into oblivion as another succeeds. So individual tides and days bring on a compressed scale the flow of the seasons as one slips into another. Even the weather changes can be seen as tidal shifts. The base, scuffed earth of scorching yesterday is today trembling with droplets condensed from the blowing wind. Refreshed and fragrant, re-born, now dotted with the corkscrew spikes of tiny green orchid and with its snailfleet skimming the film of water. From such tiny incidents as a glow-worm riding a snail's back, biding its time until it chooses to inject its host and draw out sustenance for its own life, to the majestic thunder of sea mixing with lofty cliffs.

I believe that in an appreciation of life on earth there is a rich sympathy to be felt and in it a world which runs parallel to, yet regardless of, the affairs of man, offering models that match something in our range of experience. Extending our awareness to this lends meaning to man's efforts and mundane failings, to his bereavements and his distress.

So the earth we tread is no mere setting to our endeavours but rather it is the larger fabric that contains us as one element amid its potential, and our behaviour and even our thinking modes are but elaborations of existing patterns which can be sought and observed.

woodside gardens
The pony meadow
below the
tennis
courts

sun in a shes
pressed up against
the waving soil
in among the soft tuft of
grass.

PART TWO:
THE BUTTERFLIES

Site

Summer sun, and a blown-blue sky, yet there were no Blues or even the Speckled Woods that should be here — perhaps there was too much July wind, for there was only a White flying in a field of ragwort . . . I came across an old, dried-up pond.

Here, surrounding the depression, there was a windbreak of willow, oak and a hawthorn hedge grown lank. Dotted all around were sculptured mounds of pink bramble blossom. Here were the remains of rushes, cropped by forest ponies and hoof holes, once sucked out of mud, now caked. The dry earth was relieved with islands of buttercup and fleabane. And there, flashing about me with tremendous curiosity and dash was a Small Copper, settling on the dry earth and blowing in the wind, resettling on a white flinty pebble, iridescing and winking its rich colour, scratching its head and antennae with its forelegs. Yet this time-jewel can change back to grey and become as indistinguishable as the powdery soil on which it settles, once it closes its wings. Then you know, then you realize that you have stepped into the territory of a butterfly, on this occasion a butterfly remarkable not for its rarity but for evoking in me a glowing feeling of wide-awake nostalgia — for wildness and exquisite beauty.

For some time, I sat and watched it responding to me, to the weather and its chosen pond. The sun is clouded and she presses up against the warming soil, sheltered by soft tufts of grass. She flies up to dash at a Large White as it flutters down to feed at fleabane, out into the surrounding meadow, to feed herself from buttercups or the little flat hawkbits. Yet each time she comes back to settle close and to regard me.

As a cloud comes across she resettles on grass, open-winged, then climbs down the thin waving stem and so lowers herself, now closed, into the grass mat. The territory of a butterfly is as private a world as someone else's home — that 'place' and 'site' is as important to some other creature as it is to oneself.

Like limpets which browse about their rock-face during high tide, and yet have to return to their precise position between tides, there to sit 'high and dry' until the next high water, I wonder if it is not just such a body-sense of rightness that I feel when I return to certain places. One can even return in winter when all the vigour of life's tangle is absent — and then, if anything, the feeling is stronger.

Perhaps it is the environment sense — a sense more primitive than the usual five we employ. Perhaps this remains as a vestige in our human make-up, a sense we rarely use and so rarely feel; the sort of pull which occurs in places that are most ancient, the lanes and sites and habitation of our early ancestors. A sense of home and deep relation with its place. One's roots, and past, and origin.

So to begin any study of butterflies, we must start with the past. It is difficult in England to find anything remotely resembling virgin country; today it is almost without exception a result of man's influence. And yet parts still exist in which little change has taken place. The existence of some butterfly varieties indicates that no civilized changes have taken place during the recent past. In my intensively farmed Midland county the sight of a small colony of ringlets remaining caused me to confirm from maps that this stretch of trackway with wide verges really was an ancient drove road.

As with all wild creatures, the first part to be learned is where to find them. You can start easily enough in your own back yard or garden, especially if the lawns are not too closely mown, and the flowers not drenched with insecticide. Farther afield, take a look in your neighbourhood, and see if there is a deserted garden, or an over-grown clump of small trees. Watch as you pass on sunny days and compare it with the others in the vicinity — all too well-tended. I know of one or two neglected places and it has been galling to find butterfly life there more plentiful and richer in variety, allowed to flourish by the thicker mat of grass and wild flowers beneath the garden shrubs, than in my own.

A feature of the gardens around the older, bigger houses used to be 'wilderness'. It was here that man's love of order and symmetry was relieved by natural vegetation running riot, in fact fostered and tended sufficiently to show off natural juxtaposition to its best advantage, laced with introductions such as specimen lilies, open

44

the cock brimstone also feeding from them

11.30. Down on the track the occasional chivvy of a grasshopper
the large brown warm flies that hang above it searching hawthorns — settling on their leaves
racking themselves down to perch & dart off after another or some other fly.
Like a dragonfly
quick to chase & pursue & joining, a clot together of
2 flies — clinging together for little while still
flying before separating & going back to perch.
sharp rapidity & precision
4 – 6 of them doing this over & over again
trailing their legs prior to settling.
appears to be aggression – doesn't look like mating.
tussle in the air

running call others at the ground.
ing sideways to the body of the other
midday.
1st. butterfly seen a cock brimstone feeding in the track way

day very
& very warm
track stretches
ochre with
seeds of St John's wort
a edge of a white
with copper –
no walls.

flying gently around
seeking the
occasional flower
of yellow
toadflax

stones throw from entry
half
pper
to be
as the
s. copper –
on Wednesday
lady poder
worm

amid the tangle
of spent willowherb

a dazzling &
newly emerged tortoiseshell
turning on bramble leaf
close to warm surface of
track & rabbit dropping

in this hazy sun
this ragged & quite
turning ever so slightly
now & then.
1st white flower in the track at last & over at least

Lying flatt in the dull warmth
or feeding from bramble; brief
encounter with a cock or gatekeeper

flying up ffrom or settling in
the grass or on the brambles

70°

dull sun coming thro
cloud

A good grazed turf
supports a mix of flowers.
Ragwort, from which the gatekeepers
feed along with bramble,
hawkbit, clover, pink centuary.
mouse ear chickweed, brighteyes
self heal, fleabane thistle, woody nightshade
                tormentil, eggs & bacon
                milkwork (blue)
                cross leaved heather
                heather & bell or ling.
                meadow vetchling
                wood sage.

all gatekeepers seen at rocks
temp down to 68° & it sits very
in col

3 3o   sunshine
        back to 73°
            yellow
            spotted
            blue back
        sitting out of
        wind on cross leaved
        heather
        or on a
        gorse shoots
        of which it is
        very similar
        colours

                        Both m.b. & the gatekeeper
                        bob at the little blue

swatches of poppies and huge, oriental, shade-loving plants.

Here at the edge of the thicket, wild violets were encouraged, primrose, cowslip and anemone. It is time this fashion returned; all of us who could spare a patch would so enjoy the chance to grow a few wild flowers among native shrub and tree.

A similar situation closer to our century, but mostly an addition to the farm, was the orchard, where as a rule sufficient unmown grass was allowed to sport the occasional wild parsnip, dandelion and pink campion for the Orange Tips to thrive; then later in the summer a scrap of unscythed knapweed, nettle and thistle, sufficient to support the Tortoiseshell, Peacock and Brimstone. Now thrifty orchard-growers using present-day chemical aids to be sure of crops do so at the expense of bonus wildstock such as butterflies. But a neglected orchard, while painful to the apple-grower, is usually a favourite site for insects, even with only a few stunted trees. The long, soft grass around the trunks makes splendid haunts for Large and Small Skippers, especially when an old undisturbed drainage ditch or stream runs nearby.

It is a pity that the Peacock is not as prolific or as productive as the hive bee — it is inordinately fond of cherry blossom, and must do its fair share of pollination with legs and tongue. Wherever wild cherry blossoms in the wood, the Peacock population will be high.

Ruins, old farmhouses, and deserted buildings are usually fertile places for watching afternoon-feeding butterflies who are looking for hibernating quarters in coming winter months. The overgrown areas around such sites are also particularly rich, often with long-established plant communities and lush banks for feeding, shaded streams and crumbling walls where the ivy has grown thick.

Patches of scrubby, natural forestland provide haunts for the woodland species — Tortoiseshell, Speckled Wood, Fritillary, Comma, and White Admiral, and if you are really lucky the Wood White or Purple Emperor which I have never seen. Every country will have its own woodland species. It is of comfort to me that in studying butterflies the number of species in any one place and at any one time is rarely more than a dozen, a nicely manageable figure.

But remember that butterflies abound in places which could, by no stretch of the imagination, be called beauty spots. My own interest in butterflies began when I discovered a stretch of old railway, sheltered by woods, with plenty of dry cinders on the bed to absorb all rain, able only to support plant life that can withstand near a hen wall gone into hiding beneath a ledge of the eroded sandstone cliff - just within overhanging shade

Sun out - after 3-4 min she is out again - & sunny on a rock. Flat on the ground.

air temp 66° 3·15 ♀ common blue feeding from hop trefoil flowers

ock wall with prominent black bars scattered on ece of white paper

desert conditions. Many of these are annuals; they grow in abundance and great variety and are very attractive to common butterflies. The added attraction is the nearby garbage dump, which contributes scraps of loose paper blown by the wind, bits of rubbish brought up by children on their bicycles, occasional rat infestation, and the smell of smoke and stench.

Hardly anyone's vision of a naturalist's paradise, yet there is a greater quantity and variety of butterflies to be found here than almost anywhere in the neighbourhood.

If you can recognize the qualities which prove so attractive, they will help you to find similar places (perhaps without the smells!) near your home.

First, an area relatively undisturbed, yet with enough traffic from horses, rabbits and children to keep the undergrowth from becoming too dense and too shaded. Rabbits in particular are a kind of unmeaning predator, roughing up the ground where they scratch and eating certain grasses where butterfly eggs are laid, but they are also very useful in retaining open spaces and creating paths to and from their warrens.

Second, shelter from wind — butterflies other than the Stormcock and Grayling need warm, still places to really flourish, and this can be provided by a stand of trees, an old wall, or sometimes the concrete towers in the middle of a city, so long as weeds are not too far away.

The third requirement is warmth. And this can be created by man in the strangest places — remember that old concrete base in the middle of the forest where the adders basked. Often white pieces of scrap paper reflecting the sun will prove an attraction for a butterfly, and a pile of abandoned cars may provide a whole colony with a warm, still home.

These three qualities are worth seeking, perhaps in pleasanter surroundings, because their yield in butterflies is always high. But the species are so numerous (together with the moths, there are many thousand) and their requirements and adaptations so various that wherever flowering plants can thrive, conditions are possible for some butterfly to survive and even to succeed. Even at the North Pole, there has been a regular visitor, the Arctic Grayling, which is found from Canada around the Arctic to Norway and Finland.

In complete contrast to this species of the untouched tundra are the instances of adaptation to the most urban environment, where the Tortoiseshell has become almost as familiar a sight as the pigeon. Such groups thrive in the temporary corners where weeds and nettles grow, adapting to the city sprawl with comparative ease, and escaping the dangers of agricultural spraying in the field and

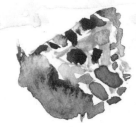

maintenance programmes on the verges along the highways. It seems funny to think of the cities as reservoirs of wild life, but this is sometimes what they are, although the majority of mammals, birds, plants and insects are peculiarly dependent on some external condition which has no city equivalent, and they must depend on national parks and pockets of untouched land for their continued existence.

Of all the butterflies I know, the Tortoiseshell, Peacock and Wall seem best suited to live with us in urban surroundings. They are greedy for warmth, and the heat radiation from brick and concrete is incomparably more comfortable than perches in open countryside. They can be seen almost all the summer long, flying on the rooftops and around the busiest streets in town, and they are to be found indoors when they go to rest for the winter, as we will see when we come to hibernation.

The Brimstone seems to be more suburban, a little more distant from us, and is commonly found in villages and small towns, feeding in churchyards and in gardens. I have been told that the Tiger Swallowtail has much the same habit, feeding on garden flowers and yet rather ignoring our presence.

The Red Admiral is a gourmet, particularly fond of squelchy, over-ripe fruit and, although it seems to be quite shy, the lure of a productive fruit or vegetable patch will bring it from quite a distance away. I have never seen either one of these species go inside a building of any kind, yet it happily negotiates fruit netting.

All of the species I have mentioned so far are fairly common within their range, and found within most countries in the temperate zone. But some species are found only in isolated pockets, usually where agricultural and climatic changes have been minimal. The Large Heath (in America sometimes called the Ringlet) must have a special sort of bogland. At the end of the Ice Age perhaps there was quite an area of upland bog where this butterfly was widespread, but now isolated pockets only are left. In each, its own colony continues to thrive and interbreed, causing slight variations from one pocket colony to the next. Should any individuals be driven out in wind and storm they perish.

Another site-dominated butterfly is called the Castle Eden Dene Blue, although it is really a sub-species of the northern Brown Argus. It lives only in a steep valley of limestone in County Durham, an ice-age pocket of ferns, lichens, mosses and a variety of other creatures which have survived since the glaciers melted. A description of the flora of that early period is now available in fair detail, culled from the pollen deposits at the bottom of lakes and bogs. Insect remains have been identified more slowly than pollen spores. It is too early to tell which butterflies, if any, were there — beetles have a hard material called chitin in their bodies and are usually preserved, but the softer butterfly structure seems less durable.

Temperature seems to be also an important factor in variation, so that sites which have different climates will develop colonies of the same species, but with intensified or lighter markings. This has been particularly well documented with the Grayling, which in spite of its strength and capacity to fly, stays in small colonies. Small Coppers, Small Whites, and Painted Ladies are also found the length and breadth of the temperate zone, but individual colonies may often

Below is a record of the nectar food plants I actually observed on the old railway line in two months of the same summer, and the species which used them. It shows two things: the range of plants and butterflies changes over a period; and if a butterfly is present for several months, it will change its food plants accordingly.

	Orange Tip	Large White	Large Skipper	Red Admiral	Brimstone	Green-veined White	Small White	Small Heath	Tortoiseshell	Meadow Brown	Small Skipper	Peacock	Small Copper	Wall
JUNE														
bramble	*	*	*	*	*	*	*		*	*				
hawkbit			*			*			*					
bird's-foot trefoil		*	*		*						*			
white clover			*											
moondaisy								*						
pink campion	*		*		*									
mouse-ear chickweed								*						
bryony							*							
red clover		*												
pyramid orchid		*												
AUGUST														
buddleia									*			*		
bramble						*								
rosebay						*	*			*				*
knapweed										*				
St John's wort										*	*			
yarrow														
hawkbit					*		*			*				*
hairy groundsel						*								
miniature willow herb						*	*	*						
creeping thistle					*	*	*			*			*	*
ragwort											*		*	

maintain fairly constant, separate identities.

As a general rule then, anywhere that offers sun, shelter, and the right food plant will support some form of butterfly life, and the particular variation of that life will be dependent on that one, special site. Life's so very much bound up with where we are, and nowhere morely clearly than in the butterfly world.

Edge of Bird Hill wood
pathway thro' the Monksilver

Peacocks, out of the wind,
flat on ground or close to
low herbage
cold cloudy afternoon

Green veined white
settled on bracken
fronds. Skies cloudy
not much chance
of clearing

Ringlet
crouching
on ash leaf
sitting out the
cool breeze

6.pm the ringlet
still sitting tight on
same leaf
Another distance
further on went up
into the trees to

Emergence

The adult stage of the butterfly begins when it emerges from its pupa case in the form of the imago, or mature insect. Emergence takes place all through the warm months, according to species, the time and the weather.

The earliest butterflies to appear are not emerging from the pupa state, but from adult hibernation. These are the large ones, the Peacocks, Tortoiseshells and Brimstones, big enough to store food in their bodies for the whole winter. When the first week of sunshine comes even as early as February or March, one or two begin to show, testing the air and temperature, sunning and feeding from the earliest rockery heathers or from dew and moisture. They must return into hibernating quarters before the sun goes and the cold night falls. During these rallies, providing they can feed, they can go in and out of hibernation as often as warm weather permits. As soon as true spring warmth begins around April, the rest of their species, slower to leave hibernation, appear.

For some days they court, then mate, then starts the life cycle of egg, larva and pupa, before the true emergence of adults occurs in July. These in turn will hibernate through the winter, to mate and die in their second year of life.

The first real emergence of young butterflies, the new season's population, takes place in April and May. The female will often be mated as soon as she has emerged, so for many species there will be a second flush in July and August. Each species has its preferred cycle, some with only one flush a year, others with two or even three, until the cold autumn weather kills off the adults, leaving eggs, larvae and pupae to overwinter in hibernating states until spring.

In general, the cocks emerge first. This is particularly noticeable in the highly territorial species, where the males must go through the

ritual of seeking out and maintaining a special territory, defending it
against other males before the hens are flying. At first, their wings are
all crumpled and compressed from the pupa case, and the butterfly
must climb up to a position free of any obstruction, and rest in the
warmth for up to half an hour. Circulation of the body fluid causes
the wings to swell. The new butterfly will hold them tightly closed
until they are hard and serviceable, since it is a very vulnerable
period, and in every species the underwing is marked for
camouflage.

   Then, if the sun is out, they are off to feed as quickly as possible,
trying out their new wings, which are so bright and untarnished,
exploring their surroundings, seeking the right nectar flowers in the
sunniest and most sheltered spot. The new cocks spend a few days
sparring and acknowledging each other, fighting for the prime sites,
patrolling the borders, and waiting for the hens. In some species it
can be as much as two weeks before the females emerge.

The female has an additional problem during her wing-swelling period, and must keep very close and still. Aside from birds who are watching avidly for dinner, the opening wings will later be a mating signal, and the poor, careless hen who spread her half-expanded wings would be spotted by impatient suitors even before she could fly. Once expanded she parts to sun, then flies to the nearest flower to feed, so joining the butterfly activity in her area, and the cocks will be alerted. Brand new and beautiful, without a mark or a scale out of place, the hen is mated before she has a chance to see what her landscape looks like.

For most species, it seems that temperature and weather conditions affect emergence, though it can take place at night. Conditions must be warm and sunny for the adult to fly, feed or mate, so if they are bad, the newly-emerged adult remains quiescent, relying on inertia and camouflage to keep it alive for more than a week. Only if there is not a single moment of sun and warmth will the adult finally succumb and die where it emerged, without ever having moved from that place.

One instance I have observed suggests an exception to the usual rule; the Scotch Argus seems to be triggered by an inner mechanism more than by external conditions. It always emerges around the end of July, and will die out by the end of August. There is no successive emergence during the season at all, so if the weather is really bad throughout that month, an entire colony can be decimated. Most other species provide for weather changes, failures, and natural calamities by spreading emergence over a period, to ensure that some survive.

The pre-emergence of cocks is related to territorial behaviour. In those species where the cocks do not defend their areas aggressively, there is no need for the sparring and fighting of the early period, and cocks and hens emerge haphazardly. This is also true of the hibernating butterflies, where neither cock nor hen has any sexual response at all until their second year.

We can see in the following chart that each species has its own programme, and it will be very useful to make such a chart of your own species and emergence times. It will show you when to look for emergence from pupa cases, and provide a standard background for those very early or very late sightings. The cycle repeats endlessly yet always slightly differently: adult, egg, larva, pupa, adult once more, and the butterfly world begins. The chart is based on my own observations.

BUTTERFLY

	NO. OF BROODS IN A SEASON	JAN	FEB	MAR	APR	MAY	JUN	JUL	AUG	SEP	OCT	NOV	DEC
Brimstone	1	»»»»	»»»»	»»»	▌▌▌▌	▌▌▌▌	▌▌▌▪	▪	▪▌▌▌	▌▌▌▌	»»»»	»»»»	»»»
Peacock	1+	»»»»	»»»»	»»»	▌▌▌▌	▌▌▌▌	▪▌▌▌	▪▌▌¹	▌▌▌▌	▌▌¹▌	»»»»	»»»»	»»»
Small Tortoiseshell	2+	»»»	»»»	▌	▌▌▌▌	▌▌▌▪	▪▌▌▌	▌▌▌▌	▌▌▌▌	▌▌¹▌	▌	»»»	»»»
Holly Blue	1+				▪▌▌▌	▌▌¹▌	▪		▌▌¹▌	▌▌▌▌			
Green-veined White	3				▪▌▌▌¹	▌▌▌▌	▌▌▌▪	▪▌▌²▌	▌▌▌▌	▌▌³▪▌	▪		
Small White	3+			▪	▌▌▌▌¹	▌▌▌▌	▌▌▌▪	▪▌▌²	▌▌▌▌	▌▌▌³	▪		
Large White	2				▪▌	▌¹▌▪▌	▌▌▌▌	▪▌▌▌	▌▌²▌	▌▌▌▌			
Orange Tip	1				▪▌▌▌	▌▌▌▌	▌▌▌▌						
Dingy Skipper	1					▪▌▌▌	▌▌▌▌						
Brown Argus	1+					▌▌▌▌	▌▌▌▌	▌▌					
Small Heath	2+					▪▌▌▌¹	▌▌▌▌	▌▌▌²	▌▌▪				
Common Blue	2+						▌▌¹	▌▌▌▌	▌▌▌²	▌²▌▌▪			
Wall	2					▪▌▌▌¹	▌▌▌▪		▌▌▌▌²	▌▌▌▌	▪		
Small Copper	2+						▌▌▌▌¹	▌▌▌▌	▌▌▌²	▌▌▪	▪		
Pearl-bordered Fritillary	1					▌▌▌▌	▌▌						
Duke of Burgundy Fritillary	1				▪	▌▌▌▌	▪						
Small Pearl-bordered Fritillary	1					▌▌▌▌	▪						
Large Skipper	1						▪	▌▌▌▌	▪				
Red Admiral	1						▪	▌▌▌▌	▌▌▌▌	▌▌▌▌	▌▌¹▌	▪	
Meadow Brown	2						▌▌▌¹	▌▌▌▌	▌▌▌▌				
Small Skipper	1							▌▌	▌▌▌▌				
Grayling	1							▪	▌▌▌▌	▌▌▌▌			
High Brown Fritillary	1							▌▌	▌▌▌▌	▌▌			
Purple Hairstreak	1								▪	▌▌▌▌			
Chalkhill Blue	1									▌▌▌▌			
Gatekeeper	1								▌▌	▌▌▌▌			
Scotch Argus	1								▪	▌▌▌▪			
Painted Lady [immigrant]									▌▌	▌▌▌▌	▌▌		
Brown Hairstreak	1									▌▌	▌		

for April–September each symbol represents a quarter of the month

▶▶ = hibernation – sightings are possible during freak sunny spells

▌▌ = occasional early or late sightings

▌▌ = main appearance

numerals refer to broods

Identification

Lepidoptera, the butterflies and moths, make up one of the insect families. There is no simple way to separate the two — each dividing line has exceptions. Most butterflies are sun-loving, day-flying, and usually brightly coloured. Most moths are night-flying, and those that breed and fly by day can be as brilliant as any butterfly — another reason for learning patterns of behaviour and identity clues rather than relying on appearance.

It is well to remember that even when you know a great deal about butterflies, there can be considerable confusion between some species, especially with dead specimens in a box. It is too late then to relate your find to its life pattern, which might establish its family immediately.

In my early butterfly days, I was visiting a research centre staffed by experienced and fully-trained lepidopterists. I asked about the Brown Argus, which is often confused with the female Common Blue, since both can be entirely brown on the top wing surface. One distinguishing mark often listed in textbooks is a little black speck in the centre of the Argus cock's forewings. During the day, students had thundered across the headland with nets and killing bottles, bringing home their 'catches', and that evening our lecturer picked out two specimens for me to compare, one Brown Argus and one Blue hen. I looked, and drew, and began to feel totally inadequate in the presence of their expert knowledge, because I was completely nonplussed. After the most careful examination, I could not see which was which. Finally I asked the lecturer for advice, and both he and his colleague came to help me. Or rather, to try and help me, since both had to admit in the end that they could not see any difference either, and perhaps they were both female Blues!

Of course, this was an extreme case — the two remain one of the most difficult species to tell apart, but if notes had been taken while they were alive, their habits, food patterns and flight characteristics would have sorted them out at once.

Collecting by sight instead of specimen has its problems, too. This is particularly true for the beginner, who finds it very difficult to get close enough to see the top wing surface anyway, much less worry about tiny specks on forewings. And it is also true that some species will never open their wings except in flight, or only momentarily during courtship or mating. So even with your textbook picture right to hand, short of killing them and opening their wings (which is *not* recommended!), how do you begin?

Over and over, we come back to behaviour as the best clue. Keep careful notes, and any doubts you may have out in the field will be resolved, if not at once, then over the next season or two. Identification without capture may seem an unnecessary chore, but make your notes on the spot, with as much detail as you can, and you will find that you have almost unintentionally begun a study of wildlife behaviour. Modern bird handbooks give 'habits' as important a role in identification as markings, but this essential ingredient is most often minimal or absent altogether in butterfly books. And you will find it easier and easier to recognize by habit without ever needing to see colouring or marking, just as an

grew tattered
also tried to
harry ♂ brim

2 sm coppers feeding
from creeping thistle
too

1 tab

/ peacock with
hind wings

82°

Buff-tip moth. Southwell.
25th. May '72

Saturday 24th. May.

2.0 p.m.

Poplar Hawk Moth.
in Wilf's garden.

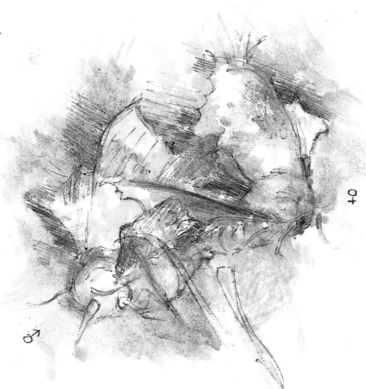

The female decided to move (like an articulated)
turned over, helping the female
ran & with her wings. She gradually
turned & crawled backwards
whilst he crawled forwards to
a plant & climbed up it &
Here they remained, still
together.

hydrangea

♀

Remained so even in
rain (not heavy)
No response whatsoever

♂

4.45 p.m.
Still in same
position.
No sign of
movement
whatsoever

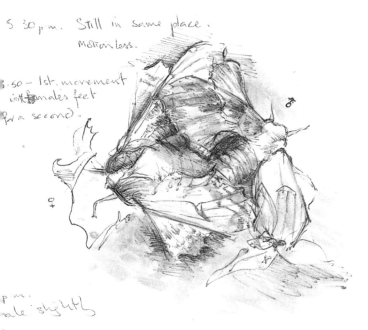

5.30 p.m. Still in same place.
Motionless.

5.50 – 1st. movement
with females feet
for a second.

♂

♀

10.30 p.m.
Dark. Parted now &
wandering inside the
glass dome which we put
on top of them. Happier
now with a poplar twig &
leaves up which they climbed
immediately.

...p.m.
...ale slightly
...less.

3.9.73.

Q.F.T. 3.5 P.M. 3rd Sept 73

warm, clouds moving fast, no sun, temp 72°
after this morning's rain.

3 s. whites
are flying
1 settled on
white umbel
the burnet saxifr

red ad. sitting on bramble leaf
among the gorse at entrance.
when sun comes out it
lifts wings, wiped its antennae
& makes off? — temp 80°
sun out

picking up again a few minutes after
lifting it from hawthorn

vegetation drying
but still beads of water
everywhere

warming
sunning during cloud
feeding at hawkbits
when sun out.

A good many of the
red abdomened drago
flies. Some chasing
each other. I think
up at passing white
cock wall.

3.50
more sun than cloud.
a sm copper sunning; with a broken
rt. hd. wing.

4.9.73. Q.F.T.
10.30 A bright sunny morning

11 Am

green-veined feeding
white deadnettle
a large white cock
bobbed at each other

orange tip ♂

green-veined-white

♀ small white

ornithologist will recognize the flight pattern of a distant bird.

Nonetheless, some knowledge of your local species and their markings is useful, to confirm behaviour patterns, and sometimes to point out a possible error in conclusions you may have drawn from field work where your notes were inadequate or patchy. And it may comfort you to know that no matter how long you have been watching and making notes, there are some species which remain confusing and awkward to identify in the wild. These can be separated into two broad groups; species in the first are impossible to tell apart at a distance, and their habits are very similar, but when seen close up, the differences are immediately clear. Examples are the Green-veined White, the Small White, and the female Orange Tip, all of which are often confused, as are the female Brimstone and the Large White. With these groups, you must make the effort to follow your insect closely until you are near enough to see them clearly.

The second group are like my female Blue and the Brown Argus, so similarly marked even if dead and pinned under a strong light that the easiest and safest identification is made by distinctive habits, *feeding on eggplant.*

"dingy skipper living up to his name. Wings well worn & chipped edges. a bewildering blur in flight as it capers about this little nooks and paths.

p.6 false oat & settling on limestone

pearl-bordered fritillary

5. p.m

A very newly emerged small-pearl-bordered frill not at all anxious to settle for night

dates or sightings, and the presence (or absence) of the larval food plant. Other species in this group are here the Pearl-bordered and Small Pearl-bordered Fritillaries and the Dark Green and the High Brown. Your local expert may be able to help you distinguish any of these groups, so a colour slide or a drawing may be particularly useful.

All over the world, the Blues are a chief source of confusion to everybody, as many vary considerably in colour, marking, size and according to sex. Just to make it worse, they may also change marking with age. When male Blues emerge, there is a beautiful white, snowy border around their gleaming wings, but if you spot one who has been around for a while, the white edge has rubbed off; considerable flying has had the effect of causing the scales to develop uneven density on the top surface, so that hints of the pattern underneath may show through. The colour changes, too, become more 'evening skyish' instead of the clear tone of the new cock. Female Blues are even more changeable, and in many common species she is not even blue — very confusing.

The following chart is a quick guide to field observers, and I recommend that you make one from your own locality as soon as you begin. These notes apply to my own area, but most of the information will be similar for other temperate zone species.

68

	Whites	Blacks	Browns	Coppers	Blues	Fritillaries	Skippers
SIZE							
male	same	smaller	smaller	smaller	same	same	smaller
female	same	larger	larger	larger	same	same	larger

note:
1. Where the sexes are the same size the abdomen of the female is plumper.
2. The difference in size is only slight.
3. In some species size can be very variable anyway.

	Whites	Blacks	Browns	Coppers	Blues	Fritillaries	Skippers
COLOUR							
male topside	same	same	darker	same	blue	same	no generalis-
underside	whiter	same	same	same	same	same	ation
female topside	same	same	lighter	same	brown	same	no generalis-
underside	yellower	same	same	same	same	same	ation

exceptions:
1. In the whites it is the Orange Tip cock which has the colour.
2. In the blues the sexes of the Brown Argus are both brown.
3. In the skippers the Large and the Lulworth are the two species
   which exhibit a difference of colour marking.

	Whites	Blacks	Browns	Coppers	Blues	Fritillaries	Skippers
SEX MARKS							
male stigma marks	nil	nil	yes	nil	nil	yes	yes

note:
These are the male stigma marks that you can see on the topside of the
wing. Even in groups where they do occur, they only do so in certain species:
examples in the browns in the British Isles are the Meadow Brown, Gatekeeper
and Wall (not the Small Heath, Scotch Argus and Marbled White); in the
fritillaries the Silver-washed only; in the skippers the Large, Small, and Essex.

	Whites	Blacks	Browns	Coppers	Blues	Fritillaries	Skippers
LEGS							
pairs	3	2	2	3	3	2	3

note:
All adult insects have three pairs of legs; there are however certain groups of
butterflies where only two pairs are seen to be used – the front pair are either
folded and small or vestigial structures.

3.30 : At Quarry . → sun ? from Lt.Wd. side. equal number ? ? to ?

4.20 . mating walks + left of the path but in the sun. couple of chasing pairs . One or 2 ? on w?

2 nd Sept
10.45
saw white
in hedgerow
feeding at lesser
bindweed + sowthistle
+ bramble

On way out of Mansfield + Pleasley
Old railway quarry
A misty start to a day of clear ?
very autumnal quiet
temp

From settled open on bramble leaves
she was disturbed by our presence.
flew off and about ? brightly
resettled on
grass .

very inal
antennae gra?
com? tog?
11.20

— white flashing
on all night
out of fore wing

otherwise
in good
condition
a lovely
purple bloom
in her

Down at road verge
where she flown + settled
within 12 inches of a sm. copper
both sent whirling away by passing van

sometimes alighting
on a thistle leaf

moving ?

back to the sun
where she opens + closes
11.45

11.55
Once settled on a warm low
wall of grass between tall
rosebay . sun partially clouded
+ getting cooler again . down to 70° .
A small froghopper . hit her . caught
the edge of her wing + she flew off

During the one hour of watching her, never once feeding !

Social life & general behaviour

In many ways, the very name 'butterfly' is a misnomer. I don't think anybody really knows its etymology, but perhaps butter was equated with the buttercup, sunshine, a sunny day. The other suggestion is that 'butterfly' is related to the colour of Brimstones, so possibly the Brimstone was the *'butter'* fly. On the other hand, the most common Brimstone is a lime green colour, so this theory does not sound very convincing to me. 'Sunfly' would be a much more accurate name for them, since they depend a great deal on the sun's cycles.

Most butterflies respond instantaneously to the absence of sun by a total cessation of activity. They hang suspended, even if caught during mating, waiting for the sun to emerge again. So necessary does this warmth and energy source seem to be that most species flying up to a bridge will shy away from its dense shadow, preferring to take the long way around by flying up and over in daylight. However, some woodland species are quite happy to fly through dappled shade.

I have been told about a Continental species of butterfly, a whitish thing, semi-transparent, with a 'solar energy pack' in its wings. If it is flying, and the sun suddenly goes in, it drops to earth immediately. It seems as though it can only launch itself into the air if it has enough energy absorbed through its 'solar pack'. That is hearsay, and I have no idea of its scientific accuracy! But in those butterflies I know well there is immediate response to the smallest change in the brilliance of the sun's light. On an overcast day, the slightest gleam, not an actual sunbeam through the clouds, but just a diffuse glow, prompts them to start feeding. The sun is an extraordinary factor in their adult lives. There are even some butterflies which seem to be able to forecast weather, rather than reacting to present conditions — these are the Orange Tips which live happily in light woodland, as long as there are glades and open spaces. There are times when I have been drawing, watching, or photographing an Orange Tip and suddenly it closes up sharply — almost snaps to! I haven't noticed any change in the weather, but when I look up to find out why it has responded, I can see the approach of the clouds, just about to obliterate the sun. Similarly, on a changeable day, in the late afternoon, it is sometimes possible to watch your butterflies taking up roosting positions earlier than usual if a large bank of clouds appears in the sky. So they seem to anticipate the change, rather than wait passively and then respond.

Temperature and light seem to be the main triggers of behaviour, but butterflies are complicated insects, with a wide variety of life patterns.

A fascinating behaviour-identification clue is the use of camouflage, both visual and through activity. Camouflage is the very basis of successful life for every species. Too often, biology textbooks take out a single instance such as colouration or posture, but the study of behaviour in the wild reveals that butterflies make use of camouflage throughout all periods of their adult life. Like many insects, they display a most amazing array of techniques developed for every purpose. Even in the caterpillar stage, colour-matching and shape mimicry have been brought to a fine art. Research has shown that the larva of the Cabbage White may take visual note of its surroundings, and may become more or less intensively marked.

Adults rely partly on the very noticeable 'eye-spots' on their wings. Tinbergen's work tested the theory that these developed to mimic hawk, owl and weasel eye patterns, so that birds flying down to pick up a possible dinner would be startled and dismayed by the much larger 'animal' that seemed to glare at them. The more life-like the eye, the more effective they are in protection, and some species even have highlights which simulate the slightly asymmetrical light reflection from the pupil. If such a focus does not scare the bird off for good, it may at least distract its attention from the most vulnerable part of the butterfly's body. This gives the insect a good chance to get away, even if a little tattered around the edges.

But the most important essential camouflage for the adult without the wing eyes is the undersurface of the wings. The Brimstones, for example, are an 'early-to-bed' species in my area, and evening for them begins around 3 or 4 p.m., even at the height of summer. They begin to flop around, obviously searching for a place to settle and hide for the night, a safe roosting-perch hidden from night-time predators. Even when I follow this conspicuous butterfly closely, it can suddenly disappear. My attention has been focused on picking up just that moment, and I go directly to where I saw it vanish and search carefully with my eyes. More often than not, I disturb it before I have actually seen it on its perch.

Up it goes again, and again I follow. It flies into the shrubby, pale-shaded leaves of the bramble and pink campion, which both have veining similar to the Brimstone itself. In a moment it is gone again, somewhere under my nose but completely hidden, tight closed on the undersurface of a leaf where it will be completely sheltered from any overnight rain. This time, on my second, third, or fourth attempt, I may be lucky. Even then, it takes a good deal of quiet attention. There are even odd little notches and nicks in the edge of the wing to make it look that much more leaf-like. As the Brimstone ages, the camouflage becomes increasingly realistic, because the scales dull down, and the slight tearing along the edges make it almost impossible to detect.

Another species not using eyes is the Orange Tip, with whom you can really play hide and seek. It favours the edge of light woodland, and rich hedges and verges. A flaming-orange tip, almost fluorescent orange, shines out like a parrot in the afternoon sunshine. I can be there, watching, taking notes, drawing while they hover over their food plants, and I know precisely where every one is — no hesitation whatever. Yet just the smallest bit of cloud near the sun, and suddenly no butterflies. The second I look up instinctively to the sun, they are gone. And as long as the sun is hidden, I will not see them until I knock the hedge bushes, and they tumble out. Their underwings have the green veining, a kind of parsley patchwork which matches the keck, or Queen Anne's lace, exactly.

Large and Small Cabbage Whites do not have that veined protection, and so they must search for roosting places among pale leaves and white flowers. You can see this comfortably in your own garden; grow Jerusalem Sage, or any silver-leaved or variegated plants, and on summer evenings, around 7 or 8 o'clock, whether you have seen them go to roost or not, tap the bushes sharply and out will come cascades of whites who thought they had found a safe perch. Night after night, they search out the most suitable backgrounds carefully. Out in the wild it is even easier to find them, since there are so many native plants and weeds with white flowerheads.

The use of signalling is principally the opposite of camouflage, and I have been asked if the opening and closing of the wings is not a kind of semaphore device, a means of communication between adult butterflies. This is a marvellous concept, and undoubtedly there is some truth in this during courtship, but except for the instances of sexual signalling, the quick opening and closing is usually a response to weather conditions or a defence.

We have already noted how quickly-closed wings may camouflage the butterfly when it searches for a roosting place, or the sun's warmth disappears. It is also employed by all hens seeking to escape notice from an unwanted cock. Even before he apparently sees her while he is flying above, a feeding hen may close down immediately and even drop into the grass to avoid recognition. This is a different response from her awareness of you as an observer, because if really disturbed, she will fly off.

Then there are all the necessary adjustments for weather, for comfort and well being. Butterflies must spread their wings just before flight to increase energy. This same sunning precedes egg-laying, and any other strenuous activity. Slow waving to and fro can sometimes be seen when conditions are too hot, usually resulting in a final close of the wings, and a stroll off under a bush to seek shelter from really intense heat. But the temperature has to be way up the thermometer before these warmth-loving creatures opt out.

In defence, the signal most commonly seen is the response to another insect too close for comfort. It seems that all species will snap shut quickly to scare off bees, hoverflies and buzzing houseflies while they are feeding. Other butterflies, moths, and bees will trigger the same response — even ladybirds and beetles if they are pollen eating on the same flower head. As usual, there are the exceptions, and John and I have seen flies settling on and crawling up butterfly wings with apparent impunity. But this is unusual, except when the butterflies are inert or during cloud. I once watched two Red Admirals in an aged hawthorn by a pond, hanging wings together, and flicking open at the flies and bluebottles which buzzed lazily around in the heat. Eventually the flies became so troublesome that one of the Admirals walked down the bark, bobbing and flicking its wings at the intruders until most of them flew away, but one stubbornly stayed right near the Admiral's head.

The Meadow Brown will flick its wings at me in the same way, but when I fail to respond by moving away, it resorts to skulking and hiding underneath the leaves.

Cocks use wing flicking as a signal to other cocks, sometimes to warn them of their presence, sometime to frighten them off if they fly down to the attack.

Finally, the wings are flicked quickly in defence to startle predators, and probably to make wing eyespots seem even more alive.

By now, midday, six
the other side. Of bo
on compost heap.
feeding close, together
Never once today has
one paid any attention
another, tho' it could
flying about the rocks
a within a few fee
a perching other.
Similarly, on the ivy
one feeds it seems obliv
- or no need to make any pl
sign of recognition or gr
to another?

speckledwood! fluttering
about golden mint
very thickly
speckled with
white —— yellow
yellow patches.

Scent

The role of scent in the life of butterflies is still quite a puzzle. From my own observations, I cannot be sure how much it affects their behaviour, because in the wild it is impossible to isolate this factor.

The most obvious effect of scent has to do with feeding. We know that certain flowers, usually those with a strong scent such as buddleias and privet, attract many species. Yet others will feed happily on mouse-eared chickweed which has almost no discernible smell at all. The sun seems to be important to the release of flower odour. But do the butterflies feed eagerly from flowers in the sun because the scent has attracted them, or because they need the sunlight to give them energy to feed? And during egg-laying some species have scent glands on their feet, and smell the surface to find the right food for their larvae. In other species the antennae serve the same function.

Scent also has an equally important but much less obvious role to play in courtship. According to Tinbergen's work on the Grayling colonies the males carry patches of scent scales on their wings. During courtship, the cock will stretch out his forewings and enclose the hen's antennae, which are rubbed up against the scent patches. Presumably this is an additional form of arousal, very necessary in this colony species. These male scent patches occur in other species as well, mostly the browns, which are colony butterflies too. I have not witnessed anything like this yet. These are all 'come hither' scents, but I have seen one of which the effect would definitely be classified as 'go-away'. This occurs as a rejection signal by the mated female. She may seek to discourage an importunate cock by various gestures, closing her wings, hiding in the grass, raising her abdomen. But sometimes this is not enough, and finally you can see her raising her abdomen and opening the genital aperture. One

77

In this instance 3.40 perching again ¾ open after sunwarmth + shy for hours, i.e. alight on a twig of hawthorn. a cock came down, fluttered strenuously over her. He failed to find her ready, she raising her tail I noticed very clearly opened the genitalia slit showing orange & it was this I believe which perhaps emit a scent as well as a language position of which made him go on, rejected

would imagine that this should have the effect of arousing the cock further, but in these circumstances it does exactly the opposite. The interior is a glistening orange. It must have a characteristic scent, because quite suddenly, the pursuing male will break off and lose interest completely. This must provide a scent barrier, since there is no other outward sign. I have noticed this can take place even in flight.

There is a great deal of further observation needed to detect both species and the activities in which, it would appear, scent is a factor used. This subject must remain largely in the hands of the professionals. Nevertheless by gathering careful observations amateurs can do much to provide clues.

Attempts at courtship do not always end in pairing.
Here is a bright sunny day in early July, where the common blue is plentiful.
Everywhere there are yellow pads of birdsfoot trefoil flowering profusely.
All together during the day there are five serious attempts seen, & not one of these
ended in pairing.   All happened between noon & 3.30 p.m.

12.5 p.m.

a wandering cock has come
across a hen, deep in vegetation

he noses her – to persuade
fluttering over her

but she closes, is unreceptive
so he climbs back to top of grasses
pauses to sun, then flies off...?

2.25 p.m.

a cock is chasing a hen
she leads him from one grass
head to another.

the waving of the grass head
makes it difficult for the
cock to manoeuvre
he touches her with his antennae.

always fluttering & settling
above her in the dominant
position, All at once he
quits & flies off...?

The fluttering courtship of one cock sometimes attracts other males to join in.

3. p.m.

Three cocks tussle before
one returns in earnest

straining to join his
abdomen with hers, curling it
over, under; seeking her receptivity

she flies up to grass, fluttering
he follows at her rear...?
suddenly he flies off...?

they wander the verges of the old railway &
feeding from the rosebay with
slightly parted wings moving
from flower to flower but too
quickly to get up to them & draw
Now & then they settle & feed from St John's
on the yellow toadflax or a bramble flower
Sometimes there are six or seven in sight then
you fail to see one

A much faster flying, newly emerged, cock wall   settled briefly, to feed on St. J. w.
got up to greet a large white

a lot of cloud & warm breeze
mostly green veined whites
very few large & small w.

tortoiseshell feeding from rosebay & St. J. w.

another
hugging the warm
cinders

its
wings
at different
[illegible] levels
according to
the cinders
beneath.
The instant the rain began
it shut
its wings

then finding it wasn't stopping
it flicked them open & closed
& walked to the herbage, tried
it under a bramble leaf

the tree
moth vo
a good de
si

her sunny on / [illegible]
leaf

another hen resting on
bramble leaf more dusk
than above & clearly
marked /veined on top
side of wing

but decided to climb up
& shelter in among
denser foliage.

Colonies & territories

Territory determines behaviour at a certain period of butterfly life, just as homemaking governs the brood period of other living beings. In species where the male actively defends territories, patrolling his borders and keeping off rival cocks, life is a continual struggle, first to obtain his territory as soon as he has emerged, then to watch for females who fly through his area, and finally to defend himself against newer and younger cocks who emerge later in the season. He will stay at his post well after the peak courtship and mating period, which is just after the hens first emerge, waiting for the occasional female who emerges later than the others. A successful cock with a good piece of real estate will keep his place almost until the end of his life. Only when there is little chance of new hens emerging will he fly free before he dies, and in species like the Small Copper, the cocks will fly considerable distances, to nearby towns and cities, resting on the sides of houses. There is little time to enjoy his freedom, though, for within a short time both cocks and hens of that brood will die off, until a fresh generation emerges. In some species it may be within a month or two, for others not until the next year.

Funnily enough, it is the smallest butterflies which are tremendously territorial-minded. Like small dogs which are always at the heels of big ones, they seem to have an extra bit of fire in their character. They are also the most aggressive cocks always scrapping with their neighbours, particularly of their own species. When the larger species come sailing by, they fly up to tumble them chasing them 500 yards or more, pushing them right out of the area. And if the visitors come back, the little cocks will return to the battle with the same enthusiasm. Only the really big hibernators seem to daunt them, and these are allowed to fly throughout the individual territories without too much resistance.

A colony of butterflies is quite different. They live in fairly close living quarters, and they do not seem to defend personal territories. Within the group area, the cocks and hens wander and flit freely, looking for food and the sunny spots. Cocks and hens emerge almost together, and the males, just a day or two older than the hens, make only the mildest sorties against other cocks.

A colony is quite compact; a botanist always knows where his plants are going to be tomorrow — they do not crawl or fly off — but few people realize that most butterfly populations are almost as resident, maintaining continual occupation of the same site. Once you have found their home, you are likely to find them year after year in the same place, even under the same leaves.

It might seem rational that a successful colony would expand, and spread into other areas, but a variety of regulating factors prevents this. The site may increase in size a little, but not very much; colonies really depend on large numbers to keep themselves going, and the important influences on future population are local conditions, predation, and disease. Cocks almost always outnumber the hens, to ensure that no hen goes unmated, and if there are too many rivals, some die off without achieving a mating, and the colony continues to maintain its equilibrium.

Recently our work has turned up something new to me, and very interesting. The hibernators, the long-lived species, only maintain a clearly defined territory for little more than a fortnight. This occurs during April, when, on any hot summer-like days, you can witness their vigorous, spiralling, courtship flights. Once pairing has taken place they no longer have need for a strictly defined territory, but the pair will stay around together in that same area for the rest of their lives. Soon after meeting the hen lays her batch of eggs in one go and thereafter they both float and fly through a very widespread home range, feeding here and there, wherever they please, oblivious of the smaller territorial borders of other species. Occasionally another cock will become aggressive, but in general these huge creatures are accepted as part of the landscape, twice the size of their neighbours, the Rolls-Royces of the butterfly world who can park in the best possible places.

Within this feeding ground, there is usually one favourite place where they can be seen alighting over and over again, often a high perch with a good all-round view. If you can spot this, there is a good chance of finding them there any day from April until June, when they begin to die off.

from dyke to same bramble bush.

80° in warm grass off track

11.15. continuous feeding
& from same berry
hardly moving except to
suck

Sm copper.
sm tot down for
a moment feeding
from rosebay

...red admirals also feeding from bramble blossom

| sm sk of edge as above wind au c (6) 8 in profusion (60) | Every - dusty dusky old skipper up to chase passing butterflies | mostly feeding from ragwort heads within its little territory for a little while carries on feeding in sun goes total over day (6) | | One cock only seen | all cocks plentiful c 30 | (2) | settled & feed in valley small white 2 on same colour & size as 2nd a high on some flowers the 1st, it flicked off to headwind to it 2' away |

The sm copper is all dash no sooner settled than up to chase something out again.

considerable energy must be spent in these skirmishes near 80° (air temp indeed)

this small copper has periods off out of its own territory

in which it settled on grasses & moves down head first fan open & feeling rapidly 'stepping' with its forefeet.

up to feed at marjoram

during cloud cooler & breezy settled closed on limestone

feeling ...
till sun ... copper ...
promptly back to its territory
duties

In general, then, there are two contrasting time scales. The smaller butterflies live only for a short time, between two and six weeks. They hold strong personal territories, or live in dense colonies, emerging, courting, mating, and dying off, all in a summer. Once mated, the hen has no relation to the cock, and continues to lay single eggs throughout the rest of her life. Whereas the hibernators are constitutionally more robust, larger, more sophisticated in structure. They emerge in July, and spend the first summer more or less alone, occupying wide but loosely defined territories which they do not seem to defend, and generally gathering energy and strength for the long winter ahead. They go to sleep in the autumn, and wake up in early spring to pair, and stay about together until they both die.

Our understanding of such social groupings in wildlife has increased immeasurably in the past few years, and a great deal of interest has been focused on the damage suffered by established colony species. We gradually begin to appreciate the balance of life-systems. Unfortunately, sometimes the inroads have been too severe to reverse the elimination of a species.

Re-establishing butterfly colonies has been tried, largely without success. A particularly interesting attempt was made with the Scotch Argus, which feeds only on a high altitude coarse plant called purple or blue moor grass. The extent of the plant is much wider than the spread of Argus colonies. There used to be a good Argus population in Yorkshire, but there does not seem to be a satisfactory reason for its disappearance. Efforts to re-establish the colony with butterflies from nearby protected cultures have failed, and the mystery remains — why does the Argus vanish in the first place, and why is it so difficult to bring back?

Records of butterfly sightings do not go back very far, and the earliest specimens I know are only about 200 years old. So it is really very difficult to make a substantial survey, related to long term changes. My conclusions are hypothetical hunches, based on my own observations.

The Scotch Argus has already been mentioned as having an inner time mechanism, which in Yorkshire means that it emerges very precisely on 28–29 July, and dies off on or around 29 August. It needs 72° if it is even to consider courtship or mating; given a few years of wet, cold August weather, an entire colony could drop to below the minimum population necessary for survival — and all without any interference from pollution or insecticide. In the

particular year that I studied, there were very few days, or even brief periods of a day, that reached the required warmth. Even if they managed to mate, then another cold spell would mean many of the females would die with hundreds of eggs inside their abdomen.

There is some evidence that our climate is gradually shifting, or at least becoming colder for a period. This might be one of the reasons that re-establishment has been so difficult. In their traditional home at high altitudes, there is plenty of cloud and rain, but also continual bursts of bright sunshine. And they only have that one month to live. . . .

I need to go back with what I learned that year and test my thoughts, to see if they are backed up by further observations over future seasonal conditions.

There is the example of re-introduction by the Nature Conservancy at Woodwalton Fen, but this is proving a full-time and continuing job. The Dutch species of the Large Copper is being bred here in large numbers, and released, every year, to boost the colony so that it retains sufficient strength to survive the rigours of the wild. No doubt they will be there as long as they are protected and supplied with food, but eventually, who knows? We can only hope, because the Copper is one of the most decorative and beautiful of the species we have destroyed.

... on, when disturbed ... skipper. flew down into grass from ... bracken where it hung upside down ... green-brown from body ... then gradually adjusted itself climbing back into grass

♀ C skipper

... rain

using her two fore legs as combs for her tongue running it time + again thro' the two fore legs held together like hands + using the proboscis for cleaning / picking up moisture + dust from the eyes + over the thorax + wings.

Disregarding the rain the butterflies are on a daisy opened to the glare of a flash of sunshine + probing busily with her tongue.

Not in the least minding the rain. Very robust + resilient.

unusually pale pearl border on topside

Weather & rain

The weather is important not only to individual butterflies, but to the welfare of the entire colony. Remembering that they are really sun-flies, one can see how rain can have an extraordinary effect on behaviour and survival.

If it is raining you can safely say there is *no* butterfly activity, and if you go out to look during bad weather you would be very lucky to find even one to watch. But if you saw one or two settle for the night, and it rains, then it is definitely worth going out the next morning to see how they fared. Most often they cling onto the underside of a leaf. Those that have recently emerged do not easily get damp, their wing-scales and body-fur act as a duck's back, the droplets are repelled and during hours of darkness a vigorous butterfly, even though in a roosting position and quiescent, is quite capable of climbing lower to seek shelter if its perch is too exposed. This is more surprising than it sounds, for only if you have touched a roosting butterfly after dusk will you know just how torpid it is and how difficult it is to get any response.

Every now and again I have seen a poor bedraggled creature that had none of the advantages of youth or a dry perch, and caught in torrential rain, it has become quite sodden. Usually these are at the end of their life span, and if not quickly dried by a sunny spell will fall foul of some predator. The damp will make them heavy, cold, and slow; unable to feed, they become even weaker, easy prey.

Yet out in summer time, walking through meadow or over the hills when the weather is muggy, I have seen flocks of little butterflies rise out of the turf, even while there is a steady drizzle. These are the Meadow Browns which are always very alert. They fly up well in advance of our approach, but quickly resettle, down in the grass. With a wink of their eyed forewings they close down, crouched and hiding.

3 p.m. we now almost obligraphy the sun
a little more breeze is gently blowing up the track
a s white is still flying the ... little green things & Δ moths on ragwort

at 1st dyke
same ♂-copper
as above topleft
the spots so large they form
a black line

as cloud
settles
it logged
into nearby
curling miniature
willow herb
walked up it
perched open

then clouds up completely
& antennae also close too

disturbed it perched ag
& opened
then lept about 8" to
bramble leaf & disappeared
perching close to the track

Often, when I am out watching, drawing and photographing, a shower overtakes me, and I can watch their reaction. Those who are very quick to respond to light change, such as the Brimstone and Orange Tip, select a perch and remain quiescent for the clouds' duration. Even that alert dynamo of energy the Small Copper will usually cease feeding and slow up, like a toy clock-work motor running down. At the onset of rain, if he has not already closed his wings, he will snap them to, and as the rain increases you will see him climbing down from the flower head. If it is big enough to afford him shelter, he will cling there upside down and await its passing.

This is common practice with all the larger species; prevented from feeding by cloudy skies, they fly down to the ground and settle with wings open to absorb the maximum radiated warmth. But as the drops start to fall, they close their wings sharply and walk off to seek the nearest shelter of thick herbage. An exception is the High Brown Fritillary who goes on feeding on bramble regardless of a shower.

I have said already that no butterfly flies in the rain unprovoked. Yet what a mistake! One spring day on the coast, the weather had been warm and sunny, yet by 4 p.m. the cloud had drifted down from the hills to envelop our protected valley. Suddenly we were

90

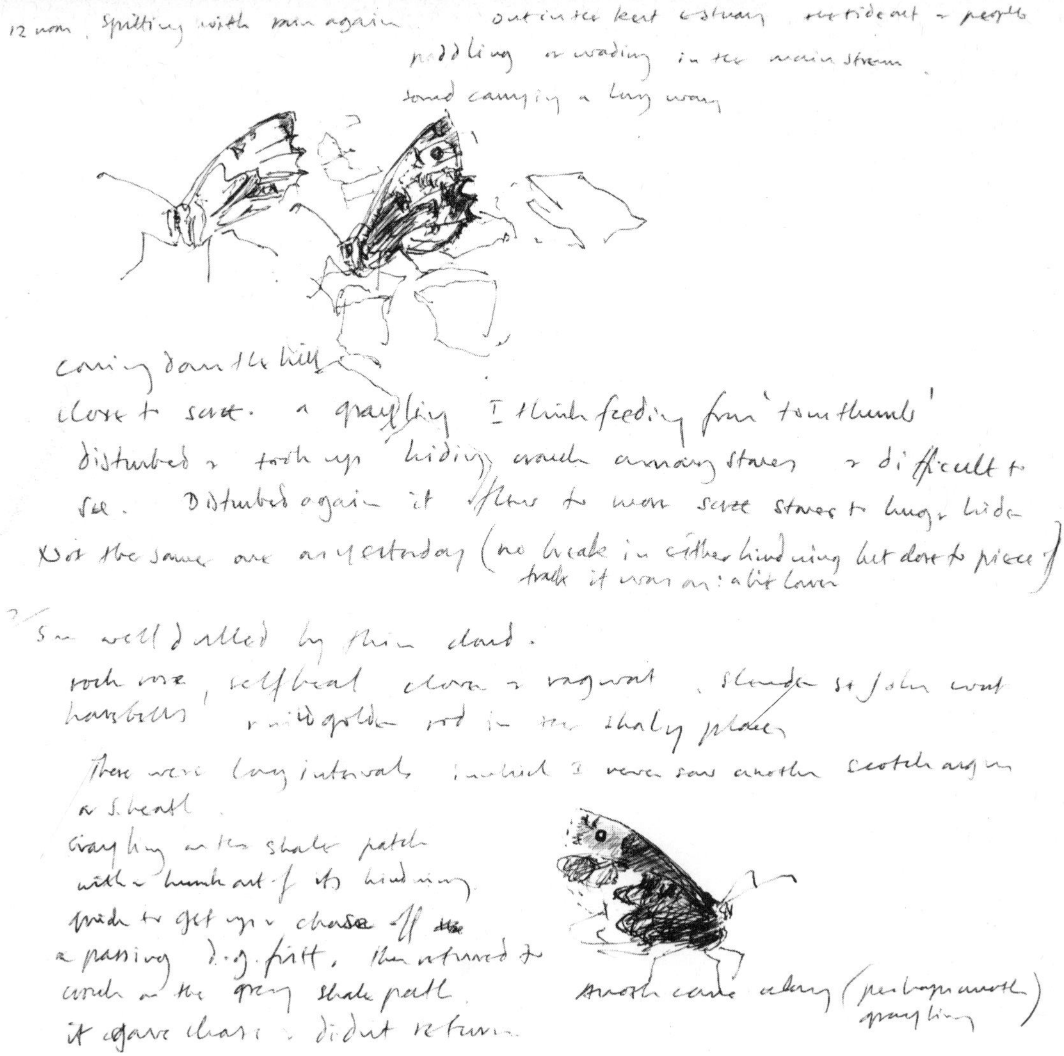
12 noon, Spitting with rain again
out in the Kent estuary the tide out – people paddling or wading in the main stream
sound carrying a long way
coming down the hill
close to scree. a grayling I think feeding from 'tom thumb'
disturbed & took up hiding crouched among stones & difficult to see. Disturbed again it flew to more scree stones to lie & hide
Not the same one as yesterday (no break in either hind wing but close to piece track it was on; a bit lower)
Sun well dulled by thin cloud.
rock rose, selfheal, clover & ragwort, slender St John wort
harebells & wild golden rod in the shaly places
There were long intervals in which I never saw another Scotch argus
or S. heath
Grayling on the shale patch
with a hunk out of its hind wing
made to get up & chase off
a passing d.g. frit, then returned to
crouch on the grey shale path
it gave chase & didn't return
Another came along (perhaps another grayling)

caught in the midst of a thunderstorm. The rain was teeming, so that we ran for the shelter of the slate porches of the lighthouse cottages and watched the ground pounded and steaming and the sandy turf and shingle paths soaking up the pouring rain. Looking out in this deluge, there, flying with vigorous sureness, skimming the steaming ground were butterflies . . . impossible to believe, contrary to all previous observations! All one kind, a grey-tinged brown: either Wall butterflies or the Dark Green Fritillary, both of which I had been watching that afternoon. Because of the darting rapidity of the flight and the slewing rain it was impossible to tell. Even forgetting the shelter of the porch and dashing out to look closer, their speed and relentless zigzag coursing was beyond me — so I could not be certain. Aside from the improbability of such a phenomenon, consider the sheer strength needed to resist the down-thrusting force of such heavy rain over such an area of wing span; what a feat!

Cent.
Old Fiskerton
track
21.6. 73
2 P.M.

the ♀ m.b. during long
interval of cloud crouched
on cinders. Sometimes disturbed
& up flying into trees by track
but always came back to perch & closed up, on ground.
sometimes moving, to clean one of the antenae.
With the flush of L.skippers in the brambles & appearance of meadow —
the miniature willowherb & pink bindweeds have come into flower.
2.15

a ♀ skipper
fanning out
like a moth,
not once doing
its bi-plane
position:
feeding from bramble flowers
1 after the other.

a slightly
, tattered
s. heath
½ way to Lot.
dyke.

A dull cock m.b.
chased & feeding
with the L. skipper
went to feed
on same bramble
flower as a ♀ sitting
quiet; she shivered
& he persisted as tho'
wishing to mate
with her! A ♂ L. skipper
came & tried to send him off
but he was unmoved &
after feeding again went back to try again!

a striped thorax & candied-bodied wasp-like
hoverfly in daudilty...

at the [...]
it begins
again

[...] quietly   waiting for the sun to reappear

Relations with other insects & the landscape

The adult butterfly is called the imago. During days when the sun is not out long enough or shining brightly and strongly enough, the imagoes wait around, and between feeding settle on the warm earth or pause to perch with wings closed on a plant — sometimes the flower from which they have been feeding — if the sun dims.

It is during such a lull in activity, when you are debating whether to move on to look elsewhere, that you notice eight or ten feet away a small cricket or froghopper eyeing the stationary butterfly. You watch it position itself, then it leaps the gap and lands adroitly on the closed wings of the butterfly. This so startles the butterfly that it invariably flies and selects another perch. It happens many times where crickets and grasshoppers abound, and with several different butterflies of different sizes, different colours and tones. Could it be just for fun — the sheer enjoyment of startling a fellow creature in your territory — just as the butterfly bobs at another and the goldfish bobs at a watersnail in his tank?

Or might it be merely a prominent and useful flat landing pad in the terrain? Grasshoppers are very carnivorous so if one were big enough this could quite well be an attempt to capture the butterfly with a view to devouring it. Crickets and grasshoppers are not the only insects to settle on the huge wing span of the butterflies. The Brimstones and Whites seem particularly beset with flies. If the weather is dull and the butterfly drowsy, the flies will alight and walk about the wing span, over the edge and on to the other side. Sometimes two will be walking about on the same butterfly's closed wing; the effect is unlike the rude arousal caused by the crickets and the butterfly will usually tolerate them — not when the sun is shining though, and activity is high. It seems, then, that bluebottles, houseflies and the like are attracted to the butterfly's proboscis.

these are creamier to brown tinged on top

Perhaps the scent of the honey nectar attracts them to suck it from the mouth parts. In any case, most butterflies will flick their wings and try to discourage their attention.

These haphazard attentions from other insects are quite distinct from the settling of red mite parasites which you sometimes see, clustered tightly about the leg/thorax, head/neck joints of butterflies. I have noticed only two kinds of butterflies troubled with these — the Marbled White and Meadow Brown. But it is likely others are too. Beetles are sometimes plagued with them.

In the wild, where there is no litter, there are several butterflies which select a bleached, curled leaf or broken stick on which to perch. Within a grassy area where a cigarette packet, matchbox or piece of silver paper show up strongly, there is one butterfly that will always select it on which to sun itself and stand sentinel within its preferred site. This is the Small Copper, with an insatiable curiosity.

From such a perch, he will hurl himself at every other passing butterfly. Whether the perch is a curled leaf or item of litter, it always offers two things: one, a dry, warm surface — the better to reflect the sun and so maintain the insect's vigour; the other, a prominent position where it can dominate.

Several other butterflies are attracted to whiteness and will settle on white paper. The Peacock, Tortoiseshell and Comma will all

come to settle on a white page if introduced in their vicinity. There are other colours attractive too, provided perhaps by a cast-off jumper, or jacket, shoes, trousers. In a different way, a scrap of white will draw a wandering white butterfly. Then during high activity it seems their greatest diversion is to find another White. Any White will do with which to twirl, and so with this in mind, they make a beeline for every white object, to see if they can 'bob' it up and fly with it. The Small White especially is a veritable busy-body, the nosey-parker of the butterfly world; not confining its attentions to other Whites it will 'set at' most of the other butterflies in its area.

My response to *Curious Naturalists* by Niko Tinbergen was immediate — as passionate a desire to know what he has to say as the best thriller can evoke. Our differences of approach are focused around our respective backgrounds; he works in the field of biology, setting up conditions and experiments, whereas I work in the field of art. To get the best drawings of the most intimate of acts in the life of an individual, I interfere as little as my presence will allow. I cannot isolate one factor to try and prove if my interpretation of events is correct or not. Instead, I can only rely on long, careful pursuit and a gradual acquisition of possible explanations for the events I see myself. But I have worked and watched carefully for a long time, and although a self-taught naturalist, I am a 'professional' observer!

So now and then, I may question his interpretations. In his early experiments with Graylings in France, an attempt was made to find what particular stimulus was required to arouse the cocks. Offering different sizes, different shapes, different colours, different tones the experimenters found that cocks will fly up at any stimulus. From this it was deduced that there is a conditioned response to everything as a sexual object.

This does not tally with my experience. It does not allow for curiosity in an insect. I would say it flies up initially to find out what is going on, and yes, it does this as much at the appearance of a human as it does to another butterfly, but then it acts accordingly.

Tinbergen also includes chasing in flight after birds as a sexual response, lumping this with the initial reaction to prospective females. Yet several species of butterflies get up and fly along with birds, and it is my guess that there is both enjoyment and a certain 'follow my leader' playfulness. Swallowtails on the Broads leap up to chase with swallows. Tortoiseshells and Peacocks around cliffs and hill tops join in their hawking flights too. A territory-patrolling Peacock will change tack to join in the flight of a pair of greenfinches, and returns when he falls behind, because he cannot keep up rather than because he has noticed that finches are not females of his own species.

Sex is not everything, and writers like Robert Ardrey have pointed out that there are many forces just as, or even more, powerful. These 'automatons' that some would have us suppose respond only mechanically, exercise a faculty of choice, exhibit remarkable memory and display signs of recognition, playfulness, zest and exultation as marked as any puppy.

I disturb a ♂ give the ♂ flying ♀ scaring the ♀ her. As they re-alight on leaf of cow parsnip another cock flutters down over them in curiosity at which the cock flaunts his wings at him.

♀

♀

♂'s close ♂ swim temp dropping to 62

Rain falling in spots. Flies climbing lower for shelter. As it strikes the leaf area of cow parsnip the 2 ♂'s shudder in sympathy to the leaf's tremor.

thunder exploding & rumbling all the clouds

All the while the stream the dyke & bubble from the little fall

temp 64

at 3.30 temp drops this doesn't stop the honey bee working in the white deadnettle nor the hoverflies at the rock. A great bumble bending down the red campion & stoneridges are beginning to attack back of my neck

3.40 As the sun shows again the two open but not for more than a minute before cloud again

4.20 & cloud coming up again looks like another rainstorm

Courtship

Before August of 1972 the importance of courtship had not seemed an exceptionally exciting field. Then, quite unexpectedly while working in a favourite area close to another old railway, I witnessed a display which was so compelling that ever since I have sought examples in the lives of other butterflies to equal it.

Before then, the idea that a Chalkhill Blue cock might go through elaborate pre-nuptials had never occurred to me; in fact I was no more interested in the pairing of butterflies than in any other aspect of their responses to each other. It was not the lack of opportunity; I had often watched Blues and Browns settled back to back, the sign of a chance to get up close and make drawings or take photographs of their undersides, for they are very torpid once settled, and consequently a little dull! The sight of one partner taking flight and carrying the other to a safer perch was always enjoyable, before it flew off as a result of my presence. But I never imagined that the preliminary courtship itself might be so spectacular. The following observations are based on the notes I made at the time.

It is four days since my last visit, studying the pattern existing between the residents of the saucer-shaped depression in the chalky bank that I call 'the dell'. With the flowering of the wild marjoram, from which all butterflies feed, and the past week's sunshine, the crickets chirp and the butterflies chase — all is activity on the bank. Everything pursues the single cock Chalkhill, and he in turn cannot resist getting up after each passing White or Brown, or even after the burnet moths, and flying grasshoppers. Could it be that he goes out of his way to be provocative? Instead of settling on a convenient head of marjoram to feed or perch on, he appears to fly over the places where the other residents would be perching, sunning, feeding, so causing the tumble and chase to be prolonged. He is obviously well known to all the other resident butterflies, who, the moment they see him flying over, are up and jogging him along, from one neighbour to the next, making it very difficult for him to alight or to feed undisturbed. Yet there seems a deal of enjoyment in the chasing. Another Chalkhill cock appears at the bank and the resident cock hurls himself at the newcomer and spins him off and away across the road out along the side road to the old track. He parades up and down the height of the bank and out across the road, towards the base of the dell, the territory of a cock Common Blue, yet the Blue seems to leave this chap well alone. He comes down to examine my white trousers and has twice almost settled on them.

Whenever a visiting butterfly appears, one of the tiny Browns and the cock Adonis join with the Chalkhill; they leave whatever they are separately doing and make a combined assault on the unsuspecting stranger, sending it well out of their territory. At the sudden appearance of a Chalkhill hen, I wonder how the three cocks will react.

For a moment she settles on the bank closest to the Chalkhill. The moment he sees her there is a lightning response and he hurls himself at her, and the Adonis and Brown Argus join in the chase and keep up with the other two. At first, it looks as though his dash was intended to send her off out of the dell, like any other intruder. How the residents take a delight in joining in the chase, the four insects gambolling in a tight cluster. They pause, and take off again up into the sky, across the road, up into the tops of ash twigs, twirling. Suddenly the hen must have left the group and got back to the bank. The male Chalkhill fails to find her so he also came back, silvery in the grass; he pauses and seems at a loss, then searching the grasses, he sees her. Flying quickly to where she perches, he perches head to head and finding her willing, then sidles with her, each trying to clasp with their abdomens. Gradually they take up a position back to back. Once joined, genitalia pulsing, they walk about or change around their position and fly a little onto a different perch, or into grass then up and back again onto the white umbel.

Pairing lasts for at least half an hour; once settled, they are not easily frightened or dislodged. They part their wings to catch the sun but then settle, inert, tight shut and not to be disturbed — so, finally, I leave them. The following day there was no sign of the hen. She will be ranging far searching for egg-laying sites. The cock is back in his territory and in his role of parading the dell. All is as before, as though nothing has happened.

Courtship begins when the cock approaches the hen. Every cock has to chase, or at least to make the approach. As a rule, it is a very active affair, fast and furious, except in the highly packed colonies,

Opposite: Small Heath on bramble blossom. The afternoon was so hot on this clay plateau that no butterflies settled for more than an instant.

Right: A cloud has obscured the sun. The Wall flew into hiding some minutes before. How well it matches with the mix of limestone, lichen, and ivy. It will roost here until tomorrow's sun.

Below: Green-veined Whites pairing on cow-parsnip. They are quite undetectable from a distance — whites make for white flower-heads to remain inconspicuous.

where the insects are so tightly grouped in their ground space that too-violent whirling and swooping might chase the hens out of their area. There is no room to stake out individual territories in the way of free-ranging males. So they have developed a much quieter form of courtship, much more ritualistic, very mild, without fire and fury. None the less, they need something to add excitement to the otherwise stabilized and rather tame form of corporate living. So the wild flight is replaced by gestures, and the swoops and swirls by quiet head-to-head rubbing, sometimes the cock's wings are put forward to shelter and enclose the female, so her antennae brush his scent glands. They bob and bow, sidling gradually against each other, until finally they are back to back, and mating can begin. For the courtship to be successful, the hen must be virgin. Since she will not mate again, the majority of attempts are towards already fertilized hens and her 'no' signal is usually enough to dissuade the cock.

Some other species rely almost on assault and battery — the cocks of the Common Wall are not tied tightly to a colony and if his frontal approach and caress of antennae is repulsed, the male will use physical coercion, bombarding the hen's wings, ramming her again and again, as though beating her into submission. The big, hibernating butterflies (the Tortoiseshell and Peacock) have a ritual of drumming on the back wings of the hen with their antennae — they will climb half onto her back, and continue drumming on her wings. Each species has developed a pattern of courtship which suits their life-style, and their physical capacity.

Of course, there are a few constants that I have observed in butterfly courtship, mostly based on physical conditions. Most important of all, the participants must have warmth and sunlight to give them enough energy and life for successful courtship and mating. The steamy warmth which follow's a night's rain is the ideal condition. Secondly courtship begins as a result of seeing the hen. Thirdly it is the cock who has to make the approach, even where the hen may be larger, or have a dominating personality. But afterwards it is a very individual matter. The courtship ritual is extraordinarily varied, but its culmination, the mating, always takes place back to back.

One of my failures has been the actual sight of Peacocks or Tortoiseshells mating, but this seems to be a failure shared by many, since I have never seen photographs or read accounts of their pairing, and certainly no one I have ever spoken to has been able to tell me of a successful courtship within eyesight. I wonder if they soar so high they mate on the wing? Always the slightly smaller cock is nosing and pushing up the soaring female, up and up in a spiral column rising a hundred feet in height. Perhaps he could cling to her and join abdomens and from then on, closed, he would hang acting like a rudder whilst she circles, throughout the mating, floating on air currents.

Does this sound far-fetched? Perhaps someone will tell me, and one day I may be there at just the right time, in the right place, with a

*shuffling their long wings if
nudged / has another or dulled*

pair of field-glasses. It has a lot to do with luck: for me this is half the
lure of working in the wild, in preference to doing controlled tests
set up in a cage. Of course you can confine your butterflies, and they
may well mate in your cage, but what of it? Out in the open, in
country, city or town, life is an unknown quantity.

My daughter Sally and her art teacher went out at lunchtime to
the edge of the playing fields for several days to watch for
Tortoiseshells during courtship, but they came back with two
different eye-witness accounts which did not quite tally. The next
day I was out with camera and notebook, and was lucky enough to
find two Tortoiseshells carrying out their courtship rituals. Sally had
said that the male had been drumming with his antennae on the back
of the female's wings, and the same thing took place with this pair. I
tried to get near enough to photograph them, but during this critical
time they are most easily disturbed — they flew as soon as I got
close. On my slides all I got of them were two specks in a mass of
ground.

I have seen a newly-emerged, unmated female next to cocks who
take no notice of her at all! Difficult to say why, except that it might
be late in the day, and the temperature so low that the cock knows it
is useless and does not even bother to start.

I have also watched a Grayling hen being mated, and fly back the
next day to lay her eggs. As she fluttered back and forth, not a single
cock showed any interest in her at all, although it was warm and
sunny. They did not even approach her to see if she was interested.
Memory, or a fluke? On the other hand, I have also seen a
magnificent, newly-emerged Large White female, mated on her first
flight as she dallied on the following day in the beauty of the
meadow, subject to further courtship attempts from every cock.

S. copper resting + sunning in warm stones, track beside cornfield

another passing + the two up + gyrating over the barley 'til it had been seen off then back + resettled

From one who refused to give up she had to hide deep in the grasses for twenty minutes.

Sometimes the sexual roles seem confused — a cock will take an interest in another cock. It does not end in pairing, of course, but a great deal of the courtship ritual can be played out until one cock uses the hen's 'no' signal, raising the abdomen, then they both lose interest and fly off. Or a cock of one species will become interested in a hen of quite a different species. This can be quite funny, particularly when they are totally different in size and habit. I watched a cock of the Large Skipper, which is actually quite small, heavy and stocky, with whirring wings, buzzing like a little aeroplane, making overtures to a great big richly-coloured Fritillary hen, much larger, with the slim butterfly shape. Perhaps it is the very contrast with his own hearty, stocky hens which attracts him. This cock must be prone to illicit overtures, for he will repeatedly approach Meadow Brown hens as well. Tit for tat, the cocks of Meadow Browns worry large Skipper females, but then these two kinds over generations of living in the same sites and in spite of their very different build, must have developed a special exchange between each other.

I have never actually witnessed a pairing between two different species, but it could only take place with closely related species. And very often, in a particularly suitable spot, in a garden or an orchard, you will see crowds of butterflies, all flying up together, like a column of mosquitoes, prompting other species to join in, chasing each other, whirling and gliding in prolongation of flight. Sometimes they seem to be clustered around a pair of Whites who are mating, pausing briefly now and then to alight on a perch and change positions and then they are off again, and the whole neighbourhood rises with them to join the party. It all happens so quickly that it is difficult to see exactly what goes on, so this is one of those occasions when a camera with its split-second exposure would be a very valuable thing.

The Skippers have a different sort of courtship pattern. The 'no' signal for the female is a violent whirring of the wings. The cock approaches from behind, and at first she whirrs away, and flies off a bit. Interestingly, the Skipper cocks will actually run across the grassheads or bramble leaves, like a water hen or road-rover, chasing the female who stops now and then to let him get near. Finally, when she is ready, she will stop and stand still. This is the signal that she is ready to accept him. He slips up beside her, then slowly they turn back to back and mate.

Skippers are the nearest relative to the moths. Moth courtship is quite different: it does not take place as a result of seeing. Structurally, many of the males have feathered antennae: this clearly demonstrates that the new-emerged female sits stationary, emitting her scent and awaiting the arrival of suitors whose fern-like appendages pick up the stimulus over long distances. Visually the closest-looking relatives of the Skipper are the burnet moths. Day-flying and with brilliant crimson spots on a green sheen, everybody notices these slow whirring creatures. To witness a perching female exuding her scent whereupon the males come flying to her from all directions, only to struggle with each other all in a desperate clamorous bid to be mate, is to witness a rather ungainly and ponderous method in comparison with any butterfly.

Again most easily disturb
-r cocks flying the hen back
into our garden chose the wa-
patch in the scarlet runner (

The cock opens left wing
the other is caught
between the fore wing
of her who remains
closed. She is in
immaculate condition
with very yellow underside.

Now she hen is trying to
open her wings, & now
pushing the cock off her hindwing.

A speck of a insect - the smallest fly (midge?)
caused no response from either & it walked
up & about between their legs.

The hen scratches & wipes her head & eyes with
both forelegs

cock stays still
(temp. 69°)

4 .5 they part

♀

4·5

4·6.

♂

Mating & after

Moths are as different from butterflies in mating as they are in courtship. Some of the larger moths have extended mating periods. In the Eyed Hawkmoth, pairing takes place in the still, dark hours of the early morning and they remain relatively quiet throughout the entire daylight hours until it is dark again, when at about 10 p.m. they part. Then, the female is straight away up and egg-laying and beginning the night's activity by depositing a few clumps on the poplar tree that she was raised on.

Pairing can take as little as twenty minutes, or as much as two hours, during which time the two insects can fly, feed, walk around, or just sit quietly. Meanwhile the male is transferring sperm from his abdomen to the hen's. The exchange however is not via a sperm fluid but takes place in the form of a capsule. This dissolves within the female cavity and contains sufficient sperm to fertilize all her eggs which explains why the female is seen to mate only once in her life. You may have to wait a long stretch of time to wait to see them part. Once they are fully sketched, noted and photographed, the only further interest for you is to watch a molesting cock drawn down to the pair out of curiosity, stimulating his desire to join in. Then you can see which of the partners is dominant, and responds defensively to the interruption.

In general, it would seem that any newly-emerged female, coming out of her case or out of hibernation, will mate if conditions are right. There has to be enough sun and warmth (a portable thermometer is a good thing to carry, by the way, it will tell you if the sun is strong enough to give you optimum conditions for courtship and mating — 72°F seems to be the lowest possible temperature for most temperate-zone species). But there are times when you notice that the female, even though newly emerged, does not draw the cock's attention.

It is important to remember, when watching butterflies mate, that the male and female genitalia, when extended, appear to be very similar, tubular constructions which lock together. Normally they are unseen, retracted within the abdomens, and only become extended during the very vigorous mating. This is always when the female is dominant and tugs and pulls the male behind her.

The curious thing is that very often the cock is dominant in flight, then once they are on the ground, it is the female who takes over dominance. Notice this is the Blue species. The cock of the Brown chases the hen aggressively, but as soon as they pair, he folds his wings and from then on she decides what will happen next. The mating of the Common Blue is staggering to watch. The hen seems to like climbing up the tall grasses, and he is dragged behind her. They are connected only by the grip of their genital parts, yet it is as though the two abdomens were one; she can pull him around as she wishes. As she gets near the tip of the grass, it bends under their combined weight, and they are rocked over and twirled about the thin stem in a circular motion, their momentum carrying them around until the hen has only to step a little further, and round they go again, every bit like a waltzer on a fairground.

He may try to ease up by flying to a different perch, but as soon as they are settled, she seeks out another long grass stem, climbs up, and round they go again! At the end of mating, the poor cock has been so wrenched around that he rests for a while with his tube extended until it is eased sufficiently to be retracted. The hen, too, is often in some discomfort and you can see her quite clearly resting *her* extended clasper tube on the surface of vegetation. Parted, they both hide for twenty minutes before entering into general butterfly behaviour. When I first watched a hen down curling her abdomen against a leaf, I thought she must be egg-laying, and it was only this year we were able to follow their courtship closely enough to realize what was taking place.

The Meadow Brown hen is a beautiful creature, velvet, soft and gloriously sure of herself. The cock, smaller and darker, is always on this mazy, hesitant flight, wavering from one stalk to another, weaving in and out of the smallest spaces between thick foliage, rarely settling — a wonderful adaptation to enable him to come across an unmated hen. For us she would be as difficult to find as a

A pair of Small Skippers in courtship in the early evening. The cock chases the hen across the grass-heads of the salt-water marshes. Her vibrating wings, her 'no' signal, dissuade him. At 6.15 he leaves her open (below), perching to sun herself.

Two views of a Speckled Wood. Newly emerged, it is in superb condition, perching in the dappled coolness of an oak-clad road.

Unless you have a male and a female side by side it is difficult to distinguish the sexes by the markings. This one is undoubtedly a cock because it flies up at everything that passes, in true territory-claiming style, and for a moment settles on my bare knee.

Left top: Orange-tip cock after a night's rain. Until he is warmed through he will be unable to move into the sun and is most vulnerable to spider predation.

Left centre: High Brown Fritillary ignoring rain and feeding from bramble flowers.

Right top: Brimstone cock on an overcast day locked on its night roost beneath a betony leaf.

Right centre, and bottom: Small Pearl-bordered Fritillary, briefly feeding on hawkbit between showers (upper picture) and showing on its underside (lower picture) the three dark blots which distinguish it from the Pearl-bordered Fritillary. It spreads to make the most of the brief moments of sun.

needle in a haystack. Meanwhile she seems to know exactly what she wants to do. After mating, she spends quite a lot of time feeding and looking for the right food plant for her eggs, and she likes to be in the company of other females. In a large clump of bramble they will choose to be together, ignoring the cocks completely and going about their business with concentration and purpose — a hen party in the proper sense. Then, all of a sudden, she seems to become quite irritated by a neighbouring female, and will go up quite aggressively to chase her off. They may have been feeding together, and even roosting close by the night before, but she will fly at her over and over again until she is successful in scaring the second female off. Then all settle down again.

The female is not always at the mercy of the cock's advance. She can be directly provocative, by playing and flirting. After a dance in the air, just as the cock has given up to rest awhile, she will come right up and nudge him flying around and enticing him to come have another twirl. Even if she has been mated, sometimes a female will lead the cock on, appearing to enjoy the ritual dance of courtship even if she will say 'no' in the end. They seem to find a good deal of fun and pleasure in chasing.

With patience, if you can wait until the natural end of the pairing, it is then that the rarely watched subsequent behaviour begins! Some butterflies leave each other without more ado, others will return and acknowledge the female. I have only once seen the female disengage first, otherwise the cock slips away, and they both usually rest for a few moments to regain strength before flying off.

Aside from these essentials, the patterns are rich and varied. It would appear to me that in some species the partners seem to share a mutual delight that goes beyond the mechanics of pairing. Sometimes I have seen the cock come back to acknowledge the female, flying over after they had separated and rested for a while, rubbing her head, and once or twice having a last twirl in the air with her before he flew off. Sometimes he even came back to see if she would respond again, but I have never seen the hen mate a second time. There are some instances when mating is interrupted by rain or they are badly disturbed by a predator, and perhaps then the hen might feel she had not received the sperm capsule to fertilize her eggs properly, but I have never seen this.

This year, in May, I saw the cock Small Heath court and mate his hen, and then separate to rest awhile. She sat quietly, in the dappled

shade of the hawthorn bush, perched on one of the leaves. Perhaps
he thought she was particularly satisfying for after about five
minutes he approached her and kept pushing at her, making short
stabs at her head and abdomen in every way appearing to begin
courtship a second time. He made a short run along the leaf. Paying
no heed to her indifference, he tried over and over again, fondling
her with his antennae, vibrating and fluttering. She made no
response, but sat more or less quietly, paying him as little attention
as possible. But when he began to knock her about by pushing with
his head and body, almost as if he would take her by force if he could,

3·25

he gathered himself for another enthusiastic try then came rushing towards her. She waited until his extended antennae were almost touching her, then neatly sidestepped. The cock could not stop — he was going much too fast, and fell clumsily off the end of the leaf to the grass below. That indignity was finally too much and he gave up. Within half an hour she had laid her first egg! That is the only time I have ever seen egg-laying happen so quickly, since it usually takes place on the following day.

Finally, the actual relationship of the male-female pair varies from species to species as much as their physical courtship patterns do. The high-density colonies do not seem to have any lasting personal interest in each other at all. There are always dozens of them about, cocks mate hens on a first come, first served basis, part, and take no notice of each other for the rest of their brief lives.

The large hibernators, in complete contrast, have the most 'loving' butterfly relationships between cock and hen. Paired for life, as they glide slowly and easily through their second summer, they will feed near each other, fly together to investigate intruders, roost nearby at night, and if one dies, or is caught by a predator, the other will remain alone until the end of its span. To see them come sailing together, down from their perch to greet you, glittering in the summer sunlight, is one of the joys of the year.

Egg-laying

Supposing weather conditions are favourable and the now mated female is ready to fulfil her special role towards the continuation of the species, usually she will spend the rest of the day (after mating) feeding, rebuffing further courtship attempts by cocks and becoming familiar with her landscape. She will roost and then next morning set about egg-laying. As in everything to do with this marvellously varied miniature world, hens of different species follow different patterns and look for different sites.

There are, of course, some common factors; laying generally takes place the day after mating, the weather must be warm enough — 70°F or more in her area and only after she has fed; then, no earlier than 10 a.m., she will look for the right food plant, so that the caterpillar, emerging about ten days later, will have proper nourishment near at hand.

Beyond these basic needs, egg-laying changes from species to species, and even from hen to hen. The actual physical act of egg laying is simple — the female puts down her abdomen, lays the egg, and then pauses for a second's rest. The number may vary from a single egg at a time to a whole raft side by side, but in all cases there is an individual action for each egg.

The first action, then, is the choice of site. Finding the right plant seems to involve a number of responses. The first is obviously vision; the hen will often zoom in from a considerable distance onto an easily recognizable plant. Scent is also important, particularly in those Cabbage Whites who love the smell of all brassica plants. The eggs, by the way, are usually laid on the leaf, not on the flower. The exceptions include the Orange Tip, who places her brick-orange eggs just beneath the white florets of the cow parsley, and by the time the egg hatches, each flower has grown into a seed pod which is

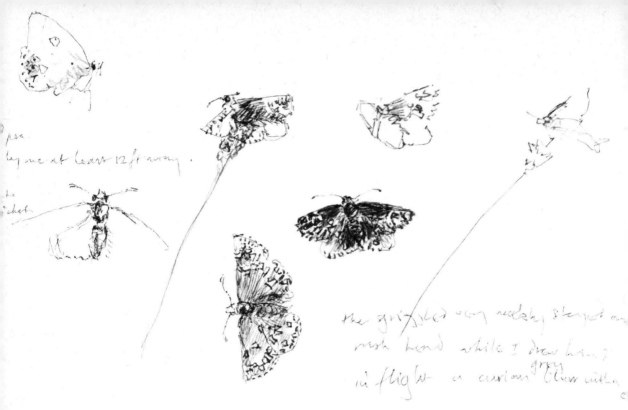

the larva's food. Another is the Holly Blue; her eggs are laid just beneath the flower so that the larva feeds on the newly-formed succulent berry instead of the tough holly leaf.

Then there seems to be a kind of prancing, a sort of lifting of the feet up and down quickly, as if to test the feel of the leaf, to make sure it is the right sort. The sense of smell may be involved here, since there are scent glands on the feet of some species. Other species use their antennae. There are some females who search endlessly throughout a meadow to find the one leaf of the one foodplant that is suitable for her egg. The Grizzled Skipper is like that, and she will spend hours looking for one tiny sprig of the cinquefoil plant. In complete contrast, the Gatekeeper hen will cling onto a piece of grass, upturn her tail, and the eggs will pop out like a cork out of a gun, falling up to 15 inches away from the laying hen, scattered around like a handful of sand blown in the wind. The large, powerful Grayling hens lay indiscriminately not only on grasses, but on bits and pieces of twig, lichen or root. So the newly-hatched caterpillar has to crawl or perish! A casual attitude for any female parent. But the hens are such stout and robust creatures themselves, perhaps they sense that their larvae have to be equally spartan and capable of survival.

The Brimstone will lay only on buckthorn and she may travel miles and miles in great leaps and bounds of flight until she finds the right place. But then she has the time, being one of the longest-living species. In a way, a distribution map of butterfly species will give you a good idea of the distribution of their food plant. The equation does not always work the other way, because there can be adverse conditions which may allow the plant to live, but not the butterfly which feeds on it.

Here is an instance where man's husbandry unwittingly provides ideal conditions for egg laying. Butterflies are sometimes not happy to lay their eggs in thickly overgrown vegetation, but prefer a stretch or even a tiny patch of grazed and flattened turf. So if a meadow has had a path mowed through it, the Meadow Browns will go immediately to that cropped area to deposit their eggs. Similarly in orchards or forestation areas, where paths have been cut between the rows for easy maintenance, Browns will gather to deposit their eggs. A hillside fire which clears a piece of woodland, and leaves a blackened, scorched patch of ashy soil is the least expected area for butterfly life. When the first few sprigs of green emerge, the Pearl-Bordered Fritillary is there to lay her eggs, and as soon as she wanders into the woodland, she returns hurriedly to her warm, sooty area.

When we pick blackberries by the hedge, and trample down the brambles, leaving crushed and trodden footprints, Small Coppers next summer will take up their territories in these hollows, and leave their eggs to fight next year's battles. Perhaps there are one or two ways in which we have countered the effects of pollution and destruction of their environment.

Sometimes, this preference for man's landscape may not please the caterpillar. Small Coppers are as apt to lay their eggs on the warm, dry cinders of my old railway track, as they are on the food plant, and the poor, newly-emerged caterpillars must go travelling to find the sheep's sorrel they need.

The eggs themselves vary from single drops like glowing pearls to dimpled 'golfballs' that can be seen quite easily. Some eggs, like those of the Common Browns, are blotched like bird's eggs, perhaps for camouflage. The Wall's green, translucent orbs are fascinating; they develop a dark, Mars-like ring at their equator, caused by the dark head of the larva. All the eggs are coated with a moist secretion when they are laid and they dry out to different degrees of firmness, depending on the species. The Tortoiseshell eggs are packed up in a coagulated pyramid, and trying to prise off a few to breed at home can be very difficult.

Hens are fairly easy to approach while laying, although photographing them in the split-second moment is difficult — you need to be quick as lightning. The number of eggs laid varies enormously. I once timed a Large White, who laid about 18 eggs in 3 or $3\frac{1}{2}$ minutes, pausing a few seconds between each deposit. If she is not disturbed, this hen will lay all her eggs at once, as will the Tortoiseshell and Peacock butterflies. In contrast, the Brimstone, having found a good patch of buckthorn will lay a single egg on each leaf tip.

If the hen is laying early in the season, the egg is laid on the tip of the bud, and as the bud grows, the egg, cemented firmly in place, rides on the unfolding leaf.

Generally speaking, the Browns are also single-laying, except for the Wall butterfly, who is the most extraordinary of the lot, following perhaps the nearest pattern to bird nesting behaviour that I have ever seen. The hen will select a favourite site, lay an egg, and then fly off. Soon she returns, just as though she was coming back to a nest, and lays the second egg next to the first. On a single thread of grass, there may be four or five eggs, laid like raindrops along the length. As they are laid at different times, there is one that hatches first. The caterpillar starts to eat immediately, and soon he has eaten quite through the blade above him, and the tip with its still-quiescent eggs falls to the ground. In this case, there really is an advantage for the first-born, since the others have to find their way back up the grass stems to reach the food.

The Blues, as a group, lay one at a time, or sometimes two. The Common Blue eggs are pale specks which become increasingly white as they dry out. Although fairly well camouflaged, when first laid, by a pale green tint, they dry to a glowing brilliance like icing. In the case of the Brown Argus, round and pitted like a tiny golfball, there can be fourteen or fifteen on one rock rose, but these will be from different females who have all found that particular plant a very suitable place for their own deposition.

The Duke of Burgundy Fritillary lays on primrose and cowslip leaves; on the underside, there may be five or six green pearls together.

Sometimes, I can see a hen perform the egg laying action over and

sequence showing a pair of Large
Whites: the male has one of his forewings
caught on the wrong side of the female's,
so that as she opens to sun she forces it
back to the closed position, although the
rest of him is trying to open. This is most
unusual.

Egg laid 24th July 1975 Lymington alburnus.

3 days old.

egg hatched by 7 am Friday 8th Aug walks quite quickly now

Green-veined white stock-side 2 Egg laid on cress leaf in turf at public park Marlborough on Aug. 2nd 75 Larva at least 2 days old so hatched either 11 or 12th.

over again, but when I search on the leaf, there is nothing. Absolutely nothing. It took me a long time to find the answer. All the single egg layers seem to run out of eggs before they give up, and so they go through the action over and over again, and the last eggs are laid sporadically.

Finally, the Large and Small Skippers, who behave in a most intelligent way. No matter how closely I watch the hen, I never see the egg after she flies off. Even picking up the grass stem after she has gone, and turning it over and over — nothing. She flies over the tuft of grass and settles on top of one. Then she shuffles backwards down and around like a woodpecker 'hutching' down a tree-trunk, then she curves her abdomen hard against the stem, stiffens, motionless, flies off. To find the eggs, you must open up the grass where it begins to furl into the stem; there, miraculously and neatly slipped into the tube, are stacked several of her translucent eggs. Now there's protection for you!

All butterfly eggs, round or flask-shaped, sculptured or smooth, translucent or opaque, have a little hole at the top called a hygrospore. If this breathing pore is submerged and the egg is left standing in water, the embryo inside will drown. So excessively wet conditions can be one of the most effective and natural population-controllers. Flooding and high tides take a particular toll of bog and coastal butterflies.

The egg-laying programme of all but the entirely batch-laying species then demands the rest of the hen's life; the average female is equipped with over a hundred eggs to deposit and only two or three weeks of life, with all its dangers, in which to carry this out.

Opposite: The sun glows through the wings of a newish female Green-veined White feeding from bramble blossom.

16·10·70   4·15 p.m. Began by being sunny & small coppers intensely
but almost at once clouded & weak & intermittent . Just inside
of the meadow , all within 15ft of each other , the central one
a plantain head , the other two feeding & moving around sl
knapweed heads

Death & predation

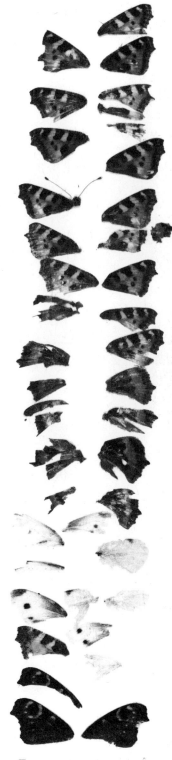

Really torrential rain, especially with a strong wind, will take a heavy toll of adult butterflies, as well as eggs caught by puddle, flood or tide. At the end of the season October frosts kill off those species that must succumb for the lack of a mechanism for hibernation. Yet following an October frost I revisited a group of Small Coppers I watched take up their roost in the grasses. As the mid-morning sunshine warmed and melted the frost from their undersides, they opened and revealed for another day their jewel-like glory. Yet every such stress caused by weather and ageing leads to a weakened state in which they are easy prey for the first hungry spider or bird.

I put spiders first as the main source of danger because in my area I would say that as much as 90% of the predation is from the spider family. It is all too easy for butterflies to be caught up in spider webs during day-time activity, and especially when they are rather torpid at night or during hibernation. Different kinds of spiders deal with their captive in different ways. Once the bite has rendered it inert, then some feed from the body where it lies, and leave the dead husk moving in the slightest wind. Other spiders roll the wings about the body and so make a neatly-trussed carcass to take back and consume in the safety of the lair.

Once I was out with Sally and Simon, and we saw a little Common Blue female fly up from feeding and touch a web; almost instantly she was caught. A huge garden spider lunged out and bit her. The butterfly immediately went limp. I hastened to tap the spider so that it retreated up to its cliff hide, yet the hen blue appeared to be already dead. I freed her from the entangling web and we popped the lifeless carcass into a plastic bag. Later in the warmth of the car she revived and we set her free amidst her kind to live again. The spider grabs and bites its victims apparently to

These remains found by Simon 26.11. 19.. beneath the ladder on the window ledge from the author

paralyse it so that without further struggle or opportunity for the butterfly to flap free, it can do as it pleases. The fact that the butterfly can recover points to the likelihood that the spider, at least this kind, injects its victim with a paralysing fluid.

Bird predation is more occasional, and seems to be an acquired taste on the part of a particular bird. Tinbergen experimented with fledglings of a wide variety of birds, from jays to yellow-hammers, and put butterflies into their cages. If they had never seen them before, then the colouration of the wings acted as a deterrent, and many of the babies would back away in alarm. But once they have realized that butterflies taste good, they will go for them again and again. You can see this yourself, if you have a part of your garden which is full of scented flowers and food plants for the butterflies. At buddleia time, there will be quite a lavish butterfly population, and the young sparrows (in my case, sparrows, but it might be any garden bird) do not seem to attack them. But in a little while, one will acquire the taste, perhaps because he finds a dead Peacock which does not struggle or flap, and then it can be wholesale slaughter. Sometimes Simon goes out to collect the wings which are left behind when the body is eaten, and there can be twenty or thirty pairs in an afternoon.

A bird that you would not think might have a fondness for butterflies is the peacock, which can gobble down the whole insect, wings and all, right down the gullet. Brownsea Island is a butterfly paradise — there is demon in the form of a very large population of semi-wild peacocks which were imported years ago and then left to breed. The result is simple; a very low number of butterflies, and a very high number of satisfied peacocks.

But peacocks are relatively uncommon, unlike pheasants which are protected and nurtured in almost every district, inhabiting every copse and wild tangle. Pheasants devour butterflies, and once they have the taste, are as avid eaters as the peacocks. Yet, as we saw when talking about camouflage, they more often go for the wing eyes instead of the body, and the butterfly gets away, though a bit worse for wear.

Cats, too, chase butterflies, being also sun-lovers and coming out gratefully into the first spring sunshine. But they seem to spend more energy in the chase than in a serious effort to catch them, particularly since the butterflies are usually flying just above the cat's reach, or in tangled bushes where the cat cannot move easily or quietly.

128

Apart from the bird and spider predation already described, and besides weather conditions, there is the ichneumon fly that attacks the larvae. Its eggs hatch into grubs which parasitize within the caterpillar skin, not inflicting any mortal wound which naturally would be disadvantageous to themselves, but coinciding their pupation with that of the caterpillars. Then, only, do they destroy the pupa, placing their tell-tale and neat double row of cocoons on the remains of the caterpillar skin.

Occasionally at the verge of the road there is evidence of a butterfly that has been dashed in collision with a car. As with birds, this form of casualty can often be the result of a heedless courtship chase up and out from the verge or hedge. These injuries, however, are not always fatal, and if you get out and rescue the inert body, after a while, in the warmth of the car, it will sometimes revive and fly off apparently as robust as ever.

On holiday at the coast you may have noticed a drowned butterfly, damaged either during migration, or from an excursion over the water when it has somehow dropped into the water, and been unable to defy surface tension over such a wide spread of wing, and slowly drowned.

Only once have I seen predation by a large wasp. It captured the butterfly in flight and carried its prey to a high perch where it devoured it. Perhaps the most bewildering occasion is when you see the butterfly one moment spread upon the grass and the next moment it has disappeared! Blink by all means, but do believe your eyes and part the grass, and there, pulled down below, is the butterfly. You may hear and glimpse the lizard predator you have disturbed scuttling away. And if you have been quick enough the butterfly with a bite out of its wings climbs back to sun, to fly off and live again.

Come what may every species seems to have its allotted span and the number of times that you witness the end of a butterfly's life is minimal when you think of the majority that disappear without trace.

The worst destroyer, of course, is mankind, with garden sprays, industry, collecting-nets and modern farming methods. Some butterflies are enormously adaptable, but if others of the most beautiful and exciting families are to survive, we must learn how to counteract the worst dangers, by making provision for them in our lives, and actively trying to create new sites when we destroy the old.

Hibernation

For some butterflies, the end of the summer is the end of an all-too-brief life. But for others, it is the signal for hibernation, the long sleep necessary for them to emerge, ready to mate and able to continue the life of their kind.

It is no accident that the hibernators are among the bigger butterflies — they have to be robust and strong to survive the long winter without food. And here, man has had a very beneficial influence. Our old buildings and cool attics in our homes are ideal places for a long winter's sleep, once they have found the right combination of temperature and relatively stable conditions.

They select a place in semi-darkness, free of draughts and avoiding extremes of temperature and humidity. Modern housing, heating and air conditioning have not left many corners, so newer houses are likely to be shunned in favour of outbuildings, garages and garden sheds. Hibernators also seem to head for the best camouflaged places, where they will blend most completely into the background. Hibernation leaves them inert and unresponsive, so that they are easily caught, and very vulnerable to spiders. Old beams are particularly favoured places, presumably since in the past butterflies hibernated in trees, as the Commas still do, and their underwing marking was adapted to the texture and shadows of bark. Brimstones still choose ivy-covered trees for their winter's perch.

Peacocks and Tortoiseshells return year after year to the same spot. Each year brings a new generation, but they enter the same houses bursting with confidence, as if they had been left a map marked with a big x. They come in generally in the afternoon as cool weather begins on a pre-hibernation inspection. They may leave there and then, or spend a trial night flying off with the sun in the morning. Finally, by the time real cold comes, they have folded their

Sitting on ceiling in bedroom. Its antennae are folded back between the wings.

As they appear 9.45 am accompanied with quivering until it becomes agitated & forewing appears when both are down. Flicks its wings open once or twice & flies directly to open slit of window & alights for a few seconds outside wings open, sunning, then i gone.

As I got closer rapidly opening closing wings. standing very upright

gust of breeze whistles along the path it sits tighter + readjust position during the [word]

Sun came out + away it went

wings, settled in a corner, ready for the winter. And there they will stay unless you have changed their environment with extra heat, electric light or the ultra-violet signals from a strip light or television set. If it is possible, catch them without harming their wings, and put them in a quiet corner out of the way, in an attic or dry basement. Then by the following night, the inertia of hibernation will most probably hold them in check until spring. I say most probably, because, like all living creatures, they surprise you most just when you think you understand their habits, and you must take a new set of factors into account.

Sometimes, a very warm sunny winter's day will make the hibernating butterfly think it is spring, and he will flap weakly at the window, trying to get out. If there really is warmth and food available, let him go, but usually it is better to give him a drop of sugar or honey dissolved in water to feed from. Then the dark night, or returning cold weather will persuade him to go back into hibernation and all will be well. It can do this any number of times, as

Opposite: More often than not the butterfly casualty on the road has been hit during a courtship chase. But this is probably not so with this Peacock, which, newly emerged in late summer, will not court until next spring, after hibernation. We found a black triangle, flat on the road surface; but as we watched, it got back on its feet, opened to gain warmth from the hot sun, and, fully revived, flew off into a garden of michaelmas daisies and dahlias.

Different butterflies feeding from the same flower: Female Gatekeeper and Marbled White (right) and Peacock (below). Wild marjoram attracts many species. Often a single head will hold several individuals.

Small Whites feeding at a variety of flowers. Top to bottom: knapweed, ragwort (left), scabious (right), primula (left), honesty (right).

long as there is food to renew its energy.

Hibernation, the suspension of life in the adult state, seems to me a remarkable ability. It is fascinating to try for yourself to assess the triggers necessary to release an individual from hibernation. This requires the testing of time, temperature and humidity, so that if you know of three or four individuals hibernating in different places it is worth watching their progress and making comparisons. Each will respond separately. Perhaps the easiest to watch is the one in your garage or shed. On a beautiful spring day throw wide the doors and watch the shaft of sun that all but touches one of these motionless black triangles. Then you will see the retracted antennae move forward, separate and vibrate fiercely. In a couple of minutes the wings of your now animated insect have opened. They too begin a rapid trembling. All of a sudden, in one jump, it has taken flight and straight as an arrow flies out into the sunshine, out into the vagaries of a new season. It is a sign for me that the lure of butterflies is beginning anew.

Opposite: A pair of Chalkhill Blues on a gorse tip. The female has a much browner underside. The cock is the larger and is dominant when in flight, but once they are both settled the female takes over the dominant role and pulls the cock behind her, very much as the Common Blue does.

Red admiral deep
in the bracken →
bramble → the
silver washed frit.
orange bomber
feeding from rosebay
flying in the glades
between hazel → the big oaks → beeches

PART THREE:
YOU AND BUTTERFLIES

In this last part of the book I want to show how you yourself may take an active interest in the butterfly life that may well be going on around you – and many of the same principles can be applied to any amateur observations of the natural world.

First, a few general hints. When selecting a site, take a fresh look at your locality and select the choice spots where shelter, sun and open areas combine. The sides of a wood and the rides within, the lanes, verges or steep banks, old railway tracks and quarries: all these are likely haunts.

Learn how to make the right approach. At first there is real difficulty in stalking. To get close enough to your insect without disturbing it calls for a different manner of walking. Do not give up; persevere and it will accept you in the end. At the same time as keeping one eye on your butterfly you need to watch for a twig that would snap, or a bramble loop or swathe of vegetation which if touched would jar and so undo all your previous care. You need to learn to glide — sharp movement will send the insect off; likewise if your shadow is cast across it. Eventually moving in the right way becomes second nature.

Such stealth especially applies to camera work. Any single-lens 35 mm reflex camera is right for the job, preferably one which has a movable standard lens so that extension tubes can be selected according to how close you want to get. Colour slides are more useful than colour negative film.

Don't make your own collection of dead specimens — give up your net and killing bottle; if and when you need to consult a collection use your local museum, or find a local expert to help.

In the next few pages we will see what positive steps can be taken to encourage butterflies to live in your garden and in your locality.

1st sunny day since
Sunday - a cold 3 days
without sun

S while roaming the garden & feeding from...

1. 30 pm

sweet rocket

The silver Y's are every...

There is very little flower left on the buddleia
& the tortoiseshells roam the garden & go back
to buddleia now & then. The settlers appear
& feed from the multiflowered white heliotropium like flowers
or on a blue bell flower. It feeds from Lobelia & a little
small yellow flower of a rock plant which it weighs heavily
to the ground

A rather broken comma (broken hind wings)
flew about the garden but went over
the hedge. A perfect spec. below
such in Colliers garden got up
& began from bushes in sun or
the night scented stock flowers.

feeding on probe...

honey...
on buddleia

This one settled on the page
as I was watching them
close to the buddleia.

They circle me as they
come down & settle on the path

on buddleia
tends to hover
feeds where...
tortoiseshell to
to take a top
where it can
the sun on its...

probing the
african
marigold
with its
greatly
extended
antennae.

Again with short
sharing its forelegs
for even with the tortoiseshell

It seems they of
tortoiseshell is quick
to start & fly
off the spike of...
only to resettle
the way.

3 pm.

7. 20 pm. the silver Y's
still in profusion;
by the river feeding
away from lobelia &
in particular the
catmint
up the garden feeding
from the pink heather & the pansies & violas.

another took cover & settled
on page.

8. 20 I at window to light.

Butterflies in your garden

Just as a pond is incomplete without waterfowl so is a garden without butterflies. No matter where you live and whether you have a roof-top patio, a back yard, or a converted barn amidst farmland, there are always butterflies to be persuaded that your patch is worth a visit. There are ways in which we can encourage their presence. One is by providing the sorts of flower food that attract them, and to some extent every garden does this. Following is a list of garden plants which I have found to be particularly effective. A good cottage-garden selection is obtainable from most seed suppliers or nurserymen. When choosing plants the rule seems that the more old fashioned the variety the more attractive they are; newer hybrids tend to be ignored in preference to the more common and original stock.

SEASON	PLANT	SPECIES ATTRACTED
spring	heathers anemone blanda aubretia yellow alyssum	butterflies from hibernation
	clematis montana sweet rocket giant allium	whites incl. Orange Tips
summer	honeysuckle	Elephant Hawk Moth
	privet	many species
	escalonia	Holly Blue
	buddleia	many species
	petunia	Bee Hawk Moth
	large African marigolds	Golden Moth, Tortoiseshell
	lavender	whites
autumn* (fall)	dahlias	Brimstone, Peacock, Tortoiseshell, Red Admiral, Painted Lady
	yellow knapweed (centaurea)	Brimstone
	Michaelmas daisy (aster)	Brimstone, Peacock, Tortoiseshell, Red Admiral, Painted Lady
	common sedum (ice plant)	Tortoiseshell
	caryopteris	Tortoiseshell
	hebe	Red Admiral, Tortoiseshell, Comma
winter	ivy flower	Red Admiral, Tortoiseshell, Comma

* Fallen fruit, such as plums, pears, apples, and overripe blackberries, is particularly attractive to the Red Admiral.

A number of foliage plants provide particularly good night protection, camouflage and shelter for the roosting butterfly. Examples are variegated dogwood, Jerusalem sage, and the grey- and silver-leaved plants such as senecios, artemisias, and centaureas.

It is true that the neatly bedded-out border makes a show, but in many respects it lacks the real beauty, the variety and continued interest of every wild, untreated meadow. Flowers such as buttercups, moondaisies, and knapweed may only last two or three weeks, but as one species dwindles another reaches its period of dominance. Each new offering occurs in the midst of the tangle of its competitors. The key to the fulsome and extravagant interest of the wild is succession, to which only the very best of gardens aspire. Most of us stick by habit or lack of time to an over-simplified, ordered tidiness with extensive bare soil between plants. Yet look at Hidcote, Sissinghurst, Nymans, Wisley and other great gardens; besides these there is usually a little garden nearer home, perhaps in a suburb, which amazes us with just these qualities of abundance, variety and succession.

Our dilemma, if we really want to encourage butterflies to breed in our garden, is that the choicest spots that we cherish for our special plants, the warmest, the most open to the sun, the most sheltered from the wind, are the very spaces most suited to butterflies' requirements. A cold, shaded corner will not do. But if you have some little area, warm and sunny, which you can afford to let grow wild it will make a good start for the common species.

Most likely you will already have two of these successfully accomplishing their life cycle unbeknown to you. The Green-veined White, in size, is similar to the small Cabbage White, but easy to recognize once settled, for the underside is marked with a green handful of fingers. And whereas the Small White and Large White lay eggs abundantly, the Green-veined White lays a single egg, in the garden, for example on rockery aubretia. Therefore the single hatched larva goes almost unnoticed on the thick mat, eating little more than one spray during its larval life before pupating. The Holly Blue is the second very important garden butterfly, and is emerged and flying in April and May. That is, if you are lucky enough to have it in your area — it is increasingly local the further north you go. It is particularly likely to occur if you have a mature holly tree with flowers — it lays its eggs on the buds and therefore goes quite unnoticed by us all. Down south it even reappears as a second brood in August when it lays its eggs on ivy flowers.

Following the example in the wild — that of competition and succession — I suggest that you grow a weed or two in among the mixed borders. A seedling or root lifted from some wild verge where a healthy colony thrives will not deplete the natural growth and will certainly enrich your offering. For the Orange Tip, include a plant of keck, pink campion and jack-by-the-hedge. What more exotic coloured spring butterfly exists? Sweet rocket needs a place too, and attracts all the family of whites to its petals, besides which its scent is invaluable. For the summer, knapweed would be a useful introduction. Try scabious and the wild marjoram, if you can get them to grow, but they like limestone. These will attract the Wall, Copper, Tortoiseshell and Peacock, to name a few. A teasel or two can be very attractive at the back of a border, and if you cut away the heads immediately the purple flowering is over (use them for winter dried flowers), another flowering will appear before the winter, and you will not get seeds all over the place.

If you have a rockery and have a space for bird's-foot there is no flower in the wild so attractive to the blue. Then there are the weeds which no gardener really wants amongst his flowers, and these could well be contained in drums or tubs and by pinching off the flowers before they seed — this will prevent trouble from the invasive varieties. I suggest dandelion, the hawkbit family, nettles and bramble.

Then instead of weeding all of the gravel path, you could use the sunny side, preferably up against a wall, for growing a crop of sheep's sorrel on which the Small Copper will breed. If you are lucky enough to have a large patch of spare grass that can be left as a hay crop or pasture, then all manner of browns and skippers, and the Common Blue, will all be encouraged.

My garden is not devoted solely to butterflies; it is as much a pleasure for me to grow flowers and vegetables as it is for others. Let me therefore assure gardeners that it is only the large and small Cabbage White butterflies that can be classed as pests. Even these I enjoy as adults, and I get rid of their larvae from my cabbages with fingers and thumb rather than by using a spray. In fact I allow the foliage of my nasturtiums to be devoured by a few of their larvae for the pleasure of watching them feed up and pupate. With these exceptions garden plants are not damaged by butterflies. My own plot is not very big and it is necessary to maximize the use of space. So the grass is mown and the beds weeded. But in these last few years I have began interplanting here and there as I have suggested, and there has been a marked increase in my butterfly visitors and the length of their stay. Now and again one of them thinks fit to deposit its egg on one of my weed offerings and I have the pleasure then of watching with relative ease the ensuing life-cycles.

To give you some guidance as to which species to expect in a given location, I have listed a number of species opposite according to their territorial habit, and in particular their degree of dependence on one place. Those that are listed under the heading 'precise location' live in one location according to the presence of a particular food plant. The foragers are more widely spread, with less well-defined territories. The immigrants (to the United Kingdom, that is) travel over much larger distances, following broadly consistent routes. Different species will be considered as immigrants or otherwise depending on where you live; but the listing opposite gives you an idea of the way you can put information together, to build up a picture of the different kinds of butterfly life in your area.

Some Species According to Territorial Habit

very precise	precise location fairly precise	foragers	immigrants
Swallowtail	Wood White	Large White	Clouded Yellow
		Small White	Bath White*
		Green-veined White	
		Orange Tip	
Purple Emperor	White Admiral	Brimstone	Painted Lady
Large Tortoiseshell		Tortoiseshell	Red Admiral
		Peacock	Monarch*
		Comma	
Mountain Ringlet	Small Heath	Wall	
Scotch Argus	Grayling		
Large Heath	Ringlet		
	Meadow Brown		
	Marbled White		
Black Hairstreak	Purple Hairstreak	Green Hairstreak	
	Brown Hairstreak		
	White Letter Hair		
Large Blue	Silver-studded Blue	Small Copper	Long-tailed Blue*
	Chalkhill (south)	Common Blue	
	Adonis	Holly Blue	
	Small Blue		
	Duke of Burgundy		
Heath Fritillary		Silver-washed Fritillary	
Granville Fritillary		Dark Green Fritillary	
Lulworth Skipper	Small Skipper	Grizzled Skipper	
Chequered Skipper	Dingy Skipper	Large Skipper	
	Silver-spotted Skipper		
	Essex Skipper		

*indicates rare visitor

grayling
settling into the
warm rock
face to the
light

Butterflies in your locality

Local administrations are often most willing and helpful in co-operating and giving advice on environmental matters. If you have the time and the energy it is a very good idea to join or even form your own local amenity group to care for and protect the character of your area. Much better management is needed to retain the natural qualities in public open spaces, footpaths, available woodland, recreational areas; perhaps one of the most significant sites from the point of view of sheer extent and variety are the verges. Local administrations may be persuaded to help local naturalists to purchase an odd corner, usually containing a pond, in order to create a small wildlife reserve. If you live in very urban conditions this could well be located in new housing developments. If it is attached to the local school it becomes important too as a natural science teaching facility. As a guide the following chart shows which wild plants need to be present if common species are to thrive in urban conditions.

Wall	larvae need soft grasses such as couch grass and foxtail	
Large Skipper Small Skipper Small Heath Meadow Brown	adults require bramble blossom and hawkbit	happier in colonies lives in colonies
Orange Tip	hedge mustard for larvae pink campion for adult feeding	
Green-veined White	(non cabbage-eating white) larvae feed on cresses including lady-smock and aubretia adults feed on many flowers including hawthorn and hawkbit	
Large and Small Whites	in wild feed on cliff brassicas and horseradish	
Common Blue Dingy Skipper	larvae feed on bird's-foot trefoil	

Brown Argus	larvae feed solely on rockrose adults particularly fond of flowers of bird's-foot trefoil	needs to establish a colony
Small Copper	larvae feed solely on sheep's sorrel adults on ragwort and hawkbit	
Small Tortoiseshell Peacock	larvae feed on common stinging nettle in wild food plant for adult ranges from dandelion and hawkbit to bramble blossom	
Day flying and very conspicuous moths	burnet — larvae feed on grasses cinnabar — larvae feed on ragwort	need to establish a colony

The success of a species depends so much on the existing conditions that the best plan is first to observe the species in its natural environment, preferably in or close to your location to find if there are ways and means of creating an equivalent. Then once all is ready introduce a few eggs laid at the local site. Watch and see if they hatch, check if the larvae look well, then wait and hope.

My local council has been most helpful with verge care and when given maps and diagrams of particular sites of existing insect colonies and plant communities, have agreed to leave those verges uncut behind the required six feet of mown grass.

On a bigger scale and with informed management a real contribution to a country's wildlife assets could be made on motorways and freeways. The existing landscaping and tree-planting schemes are often excellent but regular mowing more often keeps flower and insect life to a minimum. Wherever there are extensive verges and high banks, areas should be fenced off behind the statutory visibility mowing so that natural vegetational covering can be established with a minimum of seasonal husbandry.

Making sense of your notes

I hope that Part 2, 'The Butterflies', gives a sufficient outline for you to make some sense of what you see.

The greatest aid that I have found is to gather field observations under five headings:

1 Emergence and pre-courtship sightings
2 Courtship
3 Mating
4 Immediately after, and post-mating behaviour. This includes the egg-laying of the female and the rest of the behaviour of the cock up to —
5 End of life and predation

The next few pages show a sample of my home-made forms. This is one way in which I try to make sense of the field notes, drawings and slides. I leave this sort of 'write-up' till the end of the day or during winter months. Because I have found it impossible to contain all instances within a rigid format, rubber stamps of main headings help enormously.

If at any time an easy method of getting contact prints of the slides were to become available to the public, then I would attach these to the forms.

NAME OF BUTTERFLY	DATE	PLACE ARNSIDE	STATE OF VEGETATION
GRAYLING	11 July 1975	Yelland Stores. In sheltered stretch of limestone surrounded by wooded cover // stone wall along road	paths & thin turf cover over limestone browned & bleached with weeks of hot dry sun. Wild thyme dominant flower also eyebright, bedstraw, hawkbit

OBSERVATIONS AND CONDITIONS FOR MATING

WEATHER OR EXTERNAL CHANGES	TIME	BEHAVIOUR SEQUENCE	TEMP
A warm & very dull day. A certain amount of sun	4·55	**PAIRING DESCRIPTION** First noticed the graylings as the hen lifted the pairing cock out of the way of my approach, realighting on limestone, both closed with their wing 'eye' showing their alarm ♀ ▲ DOMINANT ▲ PARTNER ► HEN ◄	air temp around 70° during glow of sun, turf temp 75°
DISTURBED BY- As it gets cloudier	5 p.m.	RESPONSE TO- Both are side-stepping like crabs and closing down in unison, neither is dominant, mutual understanding as they turn about. - inconspicuous -	
Because of cloud a newly emerged tortoiseshell lands alongside them on same flat top of rock 4" away	5·5	— no response from either of them. (Later I find this tort. is a resident of their area therefore / known & accepted.)	
DISTURBED BY- A large bluebottle which sends off the fly.		RESPONSE TO- The hen starts, flicks her forewings high & erect, to display the two prominent eyes .	
Yet to a woodant crawling between their legs — no response .			

NAME OF BUTTERFLY	DATE	PLACE ARNSIDE	STATE OF VEGETATION
GRAYLING	11 July 1975	YELLAND STORES ditto	ditto Last few days rain as yet made little difference.

OBSERVATIONS AND CONDITIONS FOR MATING

WEATHER OR EXTERNAL CHANGES	TIME	BEHAVIOUR SEQUENCE	TEMP
Long period of cloud		ACTIVITIES DURING The pair remain fairly still on limestone It is possible to see thro the camera lens (close up) the genetalia pulsing.	on rock surface 78°
	5·25	This time it is the male who is first to suggest a turn around and so as to present me with a less frontal view. [This is no fancy of mine but even easier to watch in a single cock, who after every flight excursion often to come up in curiosity, then resettling he will turn & ratchet himself down to present a thin line only — impossible to make out as a grayling]	♂.
	5·30	Hen active, moving about & jerking the cock along behind her, showing the 1st edge of her forewing	
		pulling the cock backwards as though to take him over the edge, out of sight,	
		... but they settled on the edge hen in dominant upper position, cock downwards.	

NAME OF BUTTERFLY	DATE	PLACE	STATE OF VEGETATION
GRAYLING	11 July 1975	YELLAND STORES. ditto	ditto

O B S E R V A T I O N S   A N D   C O N D I T I O N S   F O R   M A T I N G

WEATHER OR EXTERNAL CHANGES	TIME	B E H A V I O U R S E Q U E N C E	TEMP
DISTURBED BY:- As the sun emerges	5.40	RESPONSE TO- Up she flies, very strongly huge, & settles 10ft away the cock carried inert behind her. They are both in an upright vigourous stance; she still shows her top forewing eye.	rising to 75°
Hot sun	5.50	They part. POST NUPTUAL:- While the cock walks down climbs down the rock he leaves the hen, on the pinnacle stockstill Then she relaxes, leans over & crouches to sun	temp 76°
	Duration of pairing 55 minutes +	The cock selects a little hollow & crouches — Then, both up flying. A twirl for a moment together before going seperate ways. The cock resettles on rock tonguing at moss A little later his up & resettled on white in overcover!	
	5.55	The hen flying strongly about the edges of the wooded confines, returning to the limestone promontory to settle 15 feet away from her last perch	
Sun going again	5.57	She is up again flying about the trees & lost her ....? so unsure if she returned or left the nuptual area to roost for night	
Last of sun.			

Here is another example of the sort of record you can make of your observations of one species over a season. Below are notes of observations I have made, giving the months, the wild and garden flowers selected by the Brimstone, and the time of day of the observation. There are two ranges of colours which are chiefly selected throughout the year, the yellows and the mauves; curiously these are the two colours of the butterfly and are complementary. In comparison with other species the Brimstone is a late riser and roosts early. It only feeds for a short space of time during a day; the times given often coincided with the days' only periods of sun.

MONTH	WILD FLOWERS	TIME	GARDEN FLOWERS	TIME
(from hibernation)				
April	primrose, dog violet	11.15	daffodil	12.45
	bluebell	13.30		
May	early purple orchid	10.30		
	pink campion	13.30	yellow alyssum	a.m.
June	pink campion	12.00		
	moondaisy	13.35		
	bramble flower			
	buttercup	16.00–17.30		
	bird's-foot trefoil	16.15		
July	thistle	14.00		
	red clover, bramble	14.00		
	hawkbit	14.00		
(last season's imago dies out)				
(new season's brood emerges)				
August	white convolvulus, thistle		pink phlox	11.30
	pink bramble, rosebay	12.45	fluttering at the pink	
	cont'd feeding until	14.30	of rose and petunia	11.30
	only in that meadow and		pink geranium	14.00
	followed the sun into the		buddleia	p.m.
	adjoining pasture — to			
	hawkweed, purple loosestrife,			
	buttercup, ragwort, water-			
	mint, clover, knapweed	14.30–16.00		
	pink valerian	10.30		
	branched hawkbit	11.00		
	red clover, scabious	13.20		
September	thistle	10.30	pink phlox	11.15
	yellow toadflax, white		dahlia	11.15
	sweet-rocket	12.00	red runner-bean flower	13.30
	yellow hawkbit	14.30	pink geranium	12.30–15.00
			buddleia, potentilla, orange	
			french marigold, michaelmas	
			daisy, yellow knapweed	
			(centaurea)	p.m.
October	pink campion	11.00–13.50	large spotted dahlia	
	creeping thistle	14.00	white sweet-scented lily	
	sheep's-bit scabious	11.00–15.00		
	mauve betony			
(into hibernation)				

Conclusion

If you plot over a season all your butterfly sightings you will find you have a graph of the year's sunshine. The touch of the sun brings all to life. The 'sunflies' which wait as though locked in stone wherever they are suspended, inanimate, are set free to live again by the sun's next kiss. From dull camouflage to brilliant showiness each individual provides us with a vision between these two extremes. The subtlest change in haunt brings about a corresponding adaptation in markings to produce an extraordinary blending. Change and adaptation are at the heart of existence and survival.

Every interested amateur can contribute in no matter how small a way an accurate account of these incidents. It is through your drawings and notes that experience is captured with which to make sense of observations and even sometimes make predictions. Moreover, by watching and recognizing the qualities in things outside himself man is fired with these external qualities, vitality and exultation in being.

Through work you see afresh; something you have always taken for granted can be understood and placed within the frame of a total concept. This attempt can take place in any poky corner, odd little dyke, bit of waste land. You do not need a nature reserve or wildlife park. Making sense of a landscape, a cauldron of light, drama, and emotion, requires the traditional qualities of the explorer — tenacity and endurance, and each of us can set about it in our own way.

> . . . and we'll live,
> And pray, and sing, and tell old tales, and laugh
> At gilded butterflies . . .
>
> Shakespeare, *King Lear*

Further reading

Ardrey, R. *The Territorial Imperative: Personal Inquiry into the Animal Origins of Property and Nations.* New York 1966 and London 1967 (p.b. 1969).

Bleibtreu, J. *Parable of the Beast.* London 1968 and New York 1969.

Brower, Brower and Cranston. 'Courtship behaviour of the Queen butterfly'. *Zoologica.* New York Zoological Society.

Dalton, S. *Born on the Wind.* London 1976.

Eiseley, L. *Immense Journey.* New York 1957 and London 1973.

Fabre, J. H. *Life of the Caterpillar.* London 1916.

Fairbrother, N. *New Lives, New Landscapes: Planning for the Twenty-first Century.* London and New York 1970.

Ford, E. B. *Butterflies.* London and New York 1957.

Frisch, K. A. von. *Ten Little House Mates* (trans.). Oxford 1960 and New York 1964.

Heath, J. (ed.) *Provisional Atlas of the Insects of the British Isles. Pt 1 Lepidoptera Rhopalocera Butterflies.* London 1970.

Higgins and Riley. *Field Guide to the Butterflies of Britain and Europe.* London 1970 and New York 1971.

Hoskins, W. G. *The Making of the English Landscape.* London and Baltimore 1970.

Imms, A. D. *Insect Natural History.* London 1947.

Keble Martin, W. *Concise British Flora in Colour.* London 1972.

Lorenz, K. Z. *King Solomon's Ring.* London and New York (many editions).

Newman, L. H. *Living with Butterflies.* London 1967.

Rouland, R. *Thoreau's 'Walden'. Twentieth Century Interpretations.* London and New York 1968.

South, R. *Butterflies of the British Isles.* London 1943.

Stokoe, W. J. (ed.) *Butterflies and Moths of Wayside and Woodland.* London 1945 (new ed. 1952).

Stokoe, W. J. (ed.) *The Caterpillars of the British Butterflies.* London 1944.

Tinbergen, N. *Curious Naturalists.* New York 1968 and London 1974.

Van Der Post, L. *Venture to the Interior.* London 1952 (reprint 1960) and Connecticut 1951 (reprint 1973).

Index